Praise for

THE PEOPLE PRIORITY

"This book is grounded in lived practice and intelligent observation, with insights that stick and that CEOs can return to again and again. . . . Every CEO should have this book on their desk."

—**DAVID BROWN**, leadership and performance coach for F1 world champions, global CEOs, and prime ministers

"*The People Priority* delivers real-world insights and operational tools for the most important responsibility you have as a business leader—consistently building a winning team."

—**JORGE GROSS**, Managing Partner at Trivest Partners

"A must-read for the C-suite, this book impactfully covers the full business system needed to win the war for hiring talent. . . . C-suites should read this book together, one chapter at a time, and challenge their organizations to actually execute what is outlined here in this business-critical mission."

—**ROGER ZINO**, Founder of Socratic Dialog, Board Chair, and former private equity CEO

"One of the best management books I have read. . . . The book speaks to many of the painful lessons I wish I didn't have to learn firsthand as I navigated through high-growth situations with sponsor-backed and public companies."

—**VANCE CHANG**, CFO at Dine Brands (Applebee's, IHOP)

"If you're scaling a business and want a practical, end-to-end playbook for finding and closing the right people, this is a resource you'll come back to again and again."

—**RYAN BEAL**, CEO and Founder of Dyve Biosciences

"If you are a leader in any professional domain seeking to streamline processes for identifying, employing, and amplifying talent to force-multiply, *The People Priority* is for you."

—**MIKE QUIGLEY**, US Army Special Forces (Green Beret)

"*The People Priority* treats talent acquisition with the same rigor, discipline, and strategic intent that leaders typically reserve for capital allocation or M&A. . . . This is not a book of abstract HR theory. It's a playbook for CEOs and founders who understand that people are their most important asset and want a repeatable way to build high-performing teams that actually scale."

—**MANISH MAHESHWARI**, General Partner at BAT VC
and former India Head of Twitter

"This book shows how to embed talent acquisition into your company's DNA so that attracting and retaining high performers becomes a repeatable, disciplined capability rather than a reactive scramble."

—**ROB SOBECKI**, COO of AlpacaRelay and expert mountaineer
(summited the Seven Summits)

"As a private equity investor, I look for systems that scale, not theory—and this book delivers. It combines the clarity of a manual with a modular, repeatable talent acquisition framework that works across companies, stages, and teams. . . . This is a playbook investors and CEOs can rely on to build talent advantage at scale."

—JOSH FINIFTER, Managing Director at Access Holdings

"Olympic teams don't guess on talent—they use data, discipline, and proven processes. Rohit's Talent Acquisition Funnel method brings that same rigor to business hiring, whether you're a small business owner hiring a few or running a big business hiring many."

—ANKIT SHAH, Founder and President of Sports and Performance Cardiology and Team Cardiologist for USA Swimming

"The most expensive mistake a founder can make is a bad hire. This book provides the definitive road map to ensure that never happens. . . . It transforms hiring from a guessing game into a strategic powerhouse. . . . If you want to scale fast without breaking your culture, this is your playbook."

—BALA SANKARAN, former CEO and Founder of Alpha Ori Technologies

"A rigorous, practical guide that transforms talent acquisition into a strategic advantage. This book delivers a clear methodology empowering leaders to hire smarter, build stronger teams, and drive sustained growth."

—MARK HARRISON, CEO of Australian Prostate Center

"This is the fieldwork-based leadership playbook we were never taught. Rohit delivers a clear, practical guide to building followership and attracting top talent—a no-regrets read for anyone building a team."

—PARAS MANIAR, Cofounder of Text.ai and former CEO of Bobit

"*The People Priority* connects growth strategy to the people who execute it. Real structure. Real discipline. Less guesswork, more consistency, and a team built to perform. I've used Rohit's Talent Acquisition Funnel to build my leadership team, and it delivers."

—RENEE RUMP, CEO of Heads Up Technologies

"For anyone leading, investing in, or acquiring a business, this is a must-read. Have your leadership team read it and spend time discussing its implications for your strategy and people decisions over the coming year."

—GREG WILLSEY, CEO of Venice Brands and private equity investor and operator

"*The People Priority* conveys what it takes many leaders decades to learn: Sustainable growth is built by putting people first, not as a slogan but as a disciplined operating strategy. . . . If you are responsible for building teams, as well as the culture they operate in, this book belongs on your desk."

—PAM VONA, CEO and Cofounder of the Center for Safe and Resilient Schools and Workplaces

"Rohit brings PE-level rigor and operator-level practicality to talent acquisition—because he's actually done both. . . . Don't make your next hire without reading this."

—KAROON MONFARED, CEO of BusPatrol

"This book will save you time and money. I only wish I'd had it sooner!"

—NANCY SPLAINE, Founder and CEO of Connecting Point Marketing Group

"*The People Priority* provided the strategic and operating framework we needed to move beyond 'gut-feel' hiring. It transformed our hiring process into a disciplined, scalable engine that aligns perfectly with our long-term vision."

—JOSH SKELLY, CEO of Urban Insight and Planetizen

"This book has set out proven steps and practices of a repeatable and reliable process that importantly augments instincts in talent acquisition decisions. The focus on EQ is a thread that runs through the process, which makes this methodology particularly distinctive."

—MARK VALENA, Chaiman and former CEO

"This book's focus on building an always-on talent acquisition engine, supported by a clear, funnel-based approach, turns hiring into something practical and measurable."

—PRADEEP RAMAN, Founder and former CEO of Burrow

THE
PEOPLE
PRIORITY

THE
PEOPLE
PRIORITY

THE **CEO'S BLUEPRINT** FOR WINNING TALENT ACQUISITION

ROHIT BASSI

FAST
COMPANY
Press

Fast Company Press
New York, New York
www.fastcompanypress.com

This work is being published under the Fast Company Press imprint by an
exclusive arrangement with Fast Company. Fast Company and the Fast Company
logo are registered trademarks of Mansueto Ventures, LLC. The Fast Company
Press logo is a wholly owned trademark of Mansueto Ventures, LLC.

Distributed by River Grove Books

Design and composition by Greenleaf Book Group and Brian Phillips
Cover design by Greenleaf Book Group and Brian Phillips

Publisher's Cataloging-in-Publication data is available.

Paperback ISBN: 978-1-63908-165-3

eBook ISBN: 978-1-63908-166-0

Hardcover ISBN: 978-1-63908-167-7

First Edition

CONTENTS

STAGE 3
EXECUTE

STAGE 4
CLOSE

PREFACE

I AM EXCITED FOR YOU to read this book because it means that, like me, you believe that the true secret to a company's success rests within *our people*. I believe that they are the most important assets in a business, and because of our people who show up to work every day, we have products, services, care for our customers, and an operating business. If you want to acquire the best talent for your business to build high-performing teams, unleash business growth, and have better returns on your investment, then you have found the right book. By focusing on building distinctive talent acquisition capability within your company, you will be able to consistently build high-performing teams that will not only deliver on their purpose but also increase overall capability and capacity in your organization, allowing the company to achieve more at a higher scale and speed. Having talented people in your organization ultimately results in increasing your company's enterprise value.

I prefer using the phrase *talent acquisition* instead of *hiring* or *recruiting* because *talent* rightly puts a heavier weight on people as critical assets necessary to deliver your vision and growth strategy. This is fitting because these are the talented teammates who find solutions to complex problems and unleash the growth of your business. Given the importance of people as the most important assets to the business, the word *acquisition* is also fitting because it reframes our approach toward finding the right assets for our business, and that demands a thorough and efficient due diligence process.

Early in my career, one of my mentors told me, "Recruiting is war." That phrase has stuck with me ever since. What he meant, and I agree, is that everyone is looking for the best talent out there, and they are willing to fight hard to get it. The talent supply-demand curves are often not in favor of employers, and our time to acquire is limited—which makes the process of finding, acquiring, and retaining talent incredibly difficult and extremely competitive. Implementing a way to consistently acquire top talent to build high-performing teams not only makes building companies fun and exciting but also serves as a huge competitive advantage for the company.

Talent acquisition is a universal problem. Working with business owners, CEOs and other operators, investors, and advisors around the world—some of whom are quoted in this book—solidified my view that talent acquisition affects all business types globally, from start-ups to profit-generating hypergrowth companies, those entirely independent or backed by private equity or venture capital funds, to not-for-profit organizations, agnostic of their current size or industry. While navigating periods of macroeconomic boom and economic turmoil as well as other global events, I have seen that the process of acquiring talent has only become more complex and competitive. With the talent supply continuing to be highly unpredictable as people reflect on life choices and employers become more flexible and competitive in their geographic reach, the need for an efficient, simple, consistent, and scalable talent acquisition process that can be easily implemented is more important than ever. Which is why I wanted to offer a simple, structured, comprehensive methodology with a proven set of diligence steps, tactical principles, and practical tools to help you win. My intention is to help you succeed in consistently acquiring top talent to build high-performing teams that will deliver on your growth strategy while allowing for your culture, size, type, industry, and location of your business.

Here you will find the *what*, the *why*, and the *how* to build in-house capabilities to find those individuals who meet the leadership, operating, and technical requirements of the job, fit with your company's culture, and can be someone you (based on your diligence, analysis, experience, and instincts) enjoy working with.

Development of the Talent Acquisition Funnel

The Talent Acquisition Funnel (TAF) is a structured methodology that helps companies, agnostic of their scale, stage, industry, or geography, consistently acquire top talent. It is grounded in years of field-tested operating practices with an investor mindset. Through conscious design, the TAF addresses the requirements of businesses to keep the method simple, practical, and scalable but provides the richness and detail of an M&A-style due diligence process to prioritize and evaluate the specific skills, experiences, and practices a company needs in its future employees. My journey around the concept of talent identification started when I was part of the Wharton Business School's graduate admissions team. It continued when, as a management consultant at McKinsey and Company, I became involved in their hiring processes. In both these places, I learned how *structured*, *systematic*, and *consistent* processes are foundational to finding talent at scale. As part of McKinsey's operations and private equity practices, I grew to appreciate the importance and complexities of human capital issues for scaled global organizations.

However, I started to really understand what it takes to compete for talent at the local, regional, and national level when I joined a private-equity-financed national landscaping business, previously known as ValleyCrest Companies. It had nearly 130 local branches that were essentially structured and run as individual businesses, which had to compete in their local markets for both customers and talent. These branches rolled up into approximately thirty regional business units and ultimately into one national division. My first truly operational role with them was running a local branch about a half hour's drive from downtown Philadelphia. It was a small business with less than $5 million in revenue that presented the same P&L complexities of other, bigger business units, particularly on the people topics. It is safe to say that in a fiercely tight and competitive talent supply market, a large portion of my mind- and time share was consumed by consistent challenges of staffing permanent and seasonal teams, hiring branch and account managers, and recruiting production supervisors and field employees. While the talent evaluation techniques I had observed at Wharton and McKinsey were helpful frameworks, I quickly realized that I needed a new approach to help me hire local operational talent in a small suburban town in Pennsylvania.

You see, unlike at Wharton and McKinsey, where thousands of extremely talented people are vying to get in, I was struggling to *find* people to join the tiny business I was operating. We had to hustle hard in the local communities to persuade people to even apply for the jobs, let alone come in to interview for them. Then the battle was for them to accept an offer, show up to work, safely perform their duties, and then stick around. Our hiring felt like a year-round activity, whether driven by natural seasonal aspects, business needs, or voluntary and involuntary attrition, across the organizational stack. All of this had to be done by a handful of my senior management team as we juggled the day-to-day operations. This was a key catalyst for building a simple and practical process to hire better, more efficiently, and with ample due diligence.

Soon, I took on the responsibility of national service lines and corporate functions that supported all 130 business units. At one point, my portfolio of businesses meant that my P&L responsibilities ranged from single- to triple-digit millions and a cumulative employee head count in the thousands. This gave me the opportunity to reshape several management teams of business units, service lines, corporate functions, and managerial cohorts across the company, and tackle the scaled human capital challenge for our national footprint. This is where my passion for developing standardized talent acquisition processes took flight.

Fast-forward to my life as a private equity investor, when I got the opportunity to be on the buy side, helping business owners achieve their growth aspirations. The funds typically were used to acquire founder-led profitable businesses that needed capital and expertise to help them accelerate their growth and enterprise value. These companies reminded me of the regional business units I had worked with and helped scale during my ValleyCrest days. With employee head counts generally below one hundred, these were often B2B service businesses, with strong presence in select regional markets and occasionally at the national level. At the time of purchase, these businesses typically generated somewhere between $5 million and $25 million in annual EBITDA. My goal was to identify and implement strategies to help them ideally double in size in three years. I particularly enjoyed working with incumbent CEOs, many of them founders of the businesses, to build high-performing teams, which included developing people in-house while also hiring new talent to help the company accelerate its growth and enterprise value. Unsurprisingly, the key to consistently delivering such growth rates was getting the right people to be in the right seat and join at the right time. By the end of my time at the private equity firm, I had helped reshape over half a dozen management teams, including hiring CEOs, their direct reports, and leaders in middle management roles.

Unlike at ValleyCrest, where we had implemented standardized processes across all business units and operated within one industry, the companies I was now working with had their own unique cultures, industry challenges, staffing issues, customer requirements, growth strategies, and operational needs. While the founders and CEOs had done a phenomenal job building their teams and businesses, many of them were hungry for a more systematic, scalable, and consistent approach to building their organizations. Working with companies with a wide range of capability, capacity, and capital helped me continue to build and refine my talent acquisition practices and principles. Additionally, in writing this book I also engaged with a global community of business leaders and experts to validate and refine the principles presented here.

Why I Wrote This Book

Having reflected on my experience as an operator and investor working across various parts of the private equity and private business ecosystem with global, national, regional, and local footprints, at varying scales and stages and across numerous industries, I strongly believe that to achieve growth and ROI goals, we need the right people in the right seats at the right time. I now want to help CEOs and business leaders worldwide by sharing some of the core parts of my experience and tool kit. I decided to write this book to focus on one of the critical pieces of the people puzzle when it comes to building high-performing teams and businesses: talent acquisition. When I shared the first draft of my manuscript with CEOs and investors, many of them wanted me to help them implement this methodology and develop their own bespoke Talent Acquisition Funnel that suited their culture, scale, industry, and strategic needs. This was the catalyst for the launch of my company, People Quotient (PQ), where I now work with privately held businesses, including those backed by private equity firms, to support them on leadership development, organizational design, and talent operations. The outcome from our work is the creation and retention of high-performing teams and organizations, from executive leadership to operational teams, that consistently deliver on the strategic and financial goals of the companies.

Continuing to work with CEOs and investors of privately held businesses has allowed me to further shape the TAF, helping local, regional, and national businesses worldwide across industries. TAF principles and practices have been implemented to acquire CEOs, C-suite executives, functional heads, technical experts, middle managers, and many others across the organizational stack. The versatility of the method allows companies with single-digit, triple-digit, or even higher head counts to build skilled teams to achieve their strategic and financial goals.

Every business owner eventually finds a way to hire someone on to their team. But more often than not, driven by acute need, the process is rushed, the diligence is incomplete, the steps are not repeated, or there is limited connection to the long-term strategy of the company. Having been in those shoes, I deeply appreciate the need for a methodology that is repeatable, scalable, and affordable and that ensures a strong link between where the company is today and where it strategically wishes to get to in the future. This book is intended to enable private companies to win by building their own in-house talent acquisition engine that best suits their culture, industry, and short- and long-term growth needs.

TALENT ACQUISITION

A FEW YEARS AGO, when I was working at a private equity fund, we had just wrapped up a board meeting for one of our founder-led businesses with significant potential for organic growth by entering untapped segments and geographies. The CEO and the board had just agreed to a significant revenue target for the rest of the year, and the CEO knew that he needed someone to head the sales team of half a dozen people. Those team members were excellent at their jobs, but none of them wanted a management role or had the skills to succeed in one.

As we ended the meeting, the CEO was pumped and excited to have received the board's approval of investing in his team, but he was also extremely anxious. He had signed up for a decent jump in sales, had never had a Head of Sales on his team, and knew he had to hire someone quickly—ideally, in the next sixty days—to maximize sales in the remainder of the year. Also adding to his anxiety, he did not know where to start, who would lead the search effort, how to do market diligence, or how to find someone who knew the industry and had the relevant sales experience to hit the ground running. He also wanted someone who would fit his culture, was excited to join, would accept the compensation approved by the board, and would be willing and able to leave their current job to start soon.

This situation is familiar to many CEOs and founders: You want to rapidly grow your business, but you often face a series of internal and external challenges when it comes to acquiring talent. As challenging as talent acquisition is, such a problem can be a positive leading indicator for your business—particularly if it's driven by growth needs and backed by solid employee retention levels.

The Three Cs

Acquiring talent to build high-performing teams and scale businesses is a global and evergreen problem. As is the case with all major strategic business choices, success of talent acquisition is also affected by the three Cs of a company: capability, capacity, and capital.

CAPABILITY

As a CEO, every major decision stems from your growth strategy (what, when, and how) and ties back to what you are trying to solve for in the short (twelve months) and medium (thirty-six months) terms. One of the core capabilities that drives success in talent acquisition is a clearly defined human capital strategy (the who) that is strongly linked to—if not derived from—the company's growth strategy. Some businesses that are great at execution can manage to get away with not having a well-defined short- to medium-term growth strategy, but it eventually catches up to them. Without a clear growth strategy, businesses struggle to build a detailed human capital plan that will deliver on their growth aspirations. This creates an enormous challenge where the business finds itself in reactive hiring processes, with ineffective (timing the spend, amount, and prioritization of spend) capital allocation toward people costs, resulting in operational struggles and an eventual loss of enterprise value.

A strong connection to growth strategy brings the power of clarity when it comes to who you want to hire, why, when, and for what (financial and nonfinancial) purpose. A leading indicator of lack of clarity and connection to purpose is when you see job descriptions that look like a laundry list of tasks disconnected with the role, title, and incentives. This issue is pervasive throughout the hiring practices across many organizations, but one that can be overcome relatively easily by linking back to the growth strategy of your business.

This leads us to the issue many CEOs face, which is a shortage of enough capable people in your organization whom you can trust to develop a strategic plan, derive the human capital plan, and build high-performing teams. This issue is more acutely present and visible in rapidly growing businesses where there may not be enough in-house experience in building those high-performing teams or an HR leader to take charge.

Additionally, the company may be missing a tool kit to support those who are hiring and building teams. This dual shortfall, of people and process, not only results in weaker due diligence of talent but also leads to suboptimal hiring decisions and drains the capacity of the few who have the relevant hiring experience. That often means that you or a handful of other executives end up owning talent acquisition. As the business scales, you will unintentionally become a bottleneck to the speed and volume of acquisitions. This reduced bandwidth, limited experience, or insufficient operational leverage leads to major capability constraints that slow down the hiring engine of the business.

Whether or not your team has that experience yet, simple processes can buttress your talent acquisition efforts by supporting consistent, scalable, reliable, and manageable outcomes at higher speeds.

Speaking of process, I would be exaggerating if I said all organizations have a hiring process. Even in many mature, profit-generating, growing businesses, the executive team is hyperfocused on the business at hand and engages with talent acquisition issues only as needed. As the business grows (and wants to grow) rapidly, the lack of a process designed to hire the required talent at high volume and speed with robust diligence leads to dampening growth curves and untapped market opportunities. Then there are organizations where there is a process, but it is inconsistent (within a role, across roles, across hiring managers), does not seem to scale well, or is cumbersome. In such cases, talent acquisition becomes slow and ineffective.

The lack of process becomes an even bigger pain point when you consider the consistent shifting of the supply-demand curves of the talent market. That coupled with macroeconomic forces creates an imbalance that makes it virtually impossible for a company to time their talent acquisition perfectly. This challenge gets amplified when you account for the fact that great talent has options and does not stick around in the market for long. If your company's processes are slow or inconsistent, you will frequently miss out on acquiring top talent.

While virtualization has created opportunities for employers to find talent beyond the local market, it has also created competition for you to attract new and retain existing employees. The dual challenge is an opportunity to improve both your talent acquisition and your retention capabilities.

Most companies wish for talent acquisition speed combined with deeper or richer due diligence on candidates to minimize downstream issues, such as a gap between a new employee's expected and actual performance or a cultural disconnect between the new employee and the incumbent team. The current due diligence practices of many companies can be a combination of quick, high-level conversations; limited candidate interactions with their future colleagues; a high reliance on instinctive decision-making; overindexing on speed over quality; and limited to no confirmatory reference and background checks. Each of these items reduces the quality and timeliness of meaningful insights on the candidates and makes informed hiring decisions more difficult.

To extract meaningful insights, data is a crucial but often underused asset in talent acquisition. A heavy reliance on individual interviewers' or hiring managers' preferences and biases and not enough data (behavioral, technical, or performance) can create a false positive assessment of candidate's fit. A lack of independent and unbiased data or facts reduces the ability of the hiring team to gain insights that can fundamentally change the quality and speed of decision-making.

Another factor companies find challenging and underestimate in the hiring process is that there can be a major lag between when you wish to have someone on your team and when they can actually join your team. Ideally, the right talent will transition thoughtfully with enough notice to their previous employer. But you need to build capability in the system that allows adequate flexibility in your hiring process to account for and absorb such delays and the impact it will have on your financial plans, especially if the new employee is going to have a significant financial impact on the business (e.g., executive or functional roles, product or technology development, or operational improvements).

CAPACITY

One of the most precious items in a business is the capacity to get things done. Your team's lack of capacity can derail your entire talent acquisition process.

Time is a crucial and extremely limited commodity for you as a CEO or senior executive. Running the day-to-day business while also trying to hire people can drive the majority of executives insane. Generally speaking, if your company has fewer than fifty full-time employees, there is a strong probability that you don't have the luxury of a dedicated HR person, and a handful of executives are likely stealing time from their other operational duties to hire people. Having said this, even if there is an HR person, which is more likely in bigger companies (one hundred or more full-time employees), the executive management will still be heavily involved in the more mature stages of the process. Whether reviewing every resume for a couple of minutes or interviewing each candidate for thirty minutes, the required time quickly adds up and starts to eat into running the business. The challenge for your company is to find a balance that allows these executives to build high-performing teams while also running high-performing businesses.

In addition to shortage of time, the mental capacity dedicated to developing and executing a human capital plan can be tremendously scarce. Senior business leaders (particularly C-level folks and investors) consistently express that if they are not consciously allocating mindshare to the people needs, then no one in their business is. This problem is not exclusive to small businesses. Even in businesses that have an HR team and a triple-digit (or more) employee count, the responsibility of human capital planning often sits on very few sets of shoulders. The resultant reduction in speed to action and eventual acquisition of top talent in a competitive market results in long lead times to fill roles, strain on incumbent employees, and meaningful loss in enterprise value of the business.

CAPITAL

Capital is the third of our three Cs. Budget restrictions, the outsized expectations of some candidates, and competition from other hiring companies can stifle your talent acquisition engine.

Assuming you have a formal annual budget (which isn't always the case for many businesses), your company may not know the market pricing or may be unable to match it. This can create a major disadvantage in trying to close fast on top talent and get them to join.

The expectations of your candidates, particularly in tough talent supply conditions, can be well above that market pricing—and sometimes without rationale. On the other hand, you may struggle to price roles, basing your decisions primarily on your personal views on the value of the role, driven by a lack of market data or of appreciation for what it takes to get the job done. This results in a massive disconnect between your expectations and your candidates', creating an imbalanced outcome where you either don't make an offer or you extend yourself beyond your financial means to meet your desired candidate's expectations. Either way, the result is not productive or sustainable.

Under conditions of high demand for talent, competitors with richer capital structures are likely to offer higher compensation, driving the market rates up or stealing your candidates (and employees). This further creates an unhelpful market imbalance where growth-oriented companies, despite great cultures, may not be able to compete purely based on cash compensation. The loss of good talent (retention loss) is a real concern and a painful experience for most CEOs who are trying to figure out how to offer the right incentives to avoid the cost (real and reputational) of losing that top talent while balancing capital allocation between retaining existing employees and paying market (or above market) rates for new talent. Business owners can sometimes experience tension between balancing earned distributions to self and allocating spend toward the business and employee needs. Many have learned the hard way that overindexing on self often backfires for the business in the long run, especially as it can result in delayed or "cheaper" hires or overloading a handful of incumbent employees. Any of these scenarios eventually slows down the growth, reduces your competitiveness, and lowers the value of the business.

Finally, there is a challenge of juggling opportunity costs associated with acquiring talent. On one hand, running the new talent search costs time and capital, which takes away from running the business and making money. On the other, the longer a company holds off on filling a role, the longer it will take to extract the strategic and financial benefits from that role.

No business is immune to the challenges of capability, capacity, and capital, and a majority of businesses have at least two of these three Cs in play most of the time. Talent acquisition presents a unique aspect of this interplay, as all three Cs are required to help you find the talent that can eventually alleviate the capability gaps and capacity strain on your team while generating capital by accelerating business growth. A structured, streamlined, and simple talent acquisition process not only will help permanently offset some of these challenges but will also infuse a distinct competitive advantage that will help you deliver on your strategy and growth goals.

The Talent Acquisition Funnel

The Talent Acquisition Funnel (TAF) is a people-centric strategic methodology that improves your organization's capability to consistently acquire top talent, build high-performing teams, and scale your business. It combines both strategic and tactical steps to help your company build top teams. Each stage of the TAF is designed to tie your company's overall growth strategy to its human capital plan, which eventually leads to the purposeful hiring of every single person on your team.

There are four major stages of the TAF (see figure I.1), starting with the Plan stage, in which you make company-level decisions on growth strategy, prioritize your objectives, and inform your human capital needs—leading to talent acquisition targets. The Prepare stage is when the company begins to focus its efforts at the individual job level. The Execute stage is designed to conduct detailed due diligence to narrow the field: Candidates who meet the required criteria accelerate through the funnel to the latter stages, eventually allowing

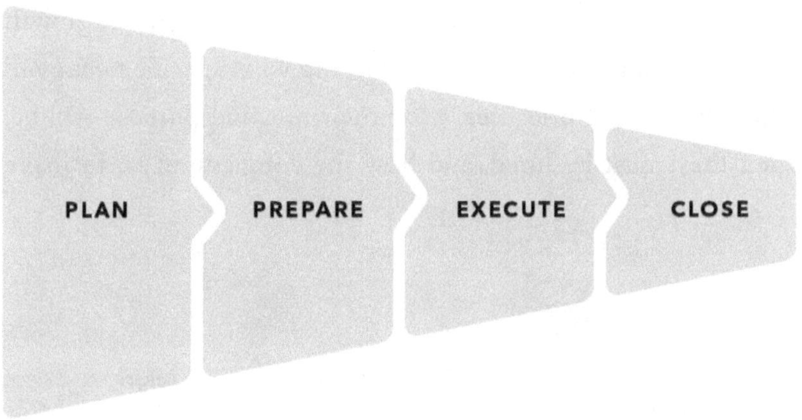

Figure I.1   The four stages of the Talent Acquisition Funnel (TAF)

the company to get to a slate of preferred top candidates. Finally, the Close stage focuses on identifying and completing the due diligence on the winning candidate, ensuring that the right employee joins your company. Each stage has specific steps that ensure strategic, efficient, thorough, and consistent talent acquisition.

PLAN

The purpose of the Plan stage (see figure I.2) is to introduce clarity to the process at the company level right from the beginning. Clarity is the single biggest weapon for success that every CEO, founder, operator, and investor needs for every single aspect of their business. Defining your strategy and knowing what you are solving for as a company prior to launching into any project, let alone one of such significance as talent acquisition, sets the foundation for your success. Clarity comes when the company uses a well-defined growth strategy (why, what, when, and how) to derive its human capital plan (who), ensuring that all hiring is strategically, operationally, and financially valuable to the organization. This is where you answer questions such as what short- and long-term growth initiatives you need to prioritize, why and what specific talent will help deliver those priorities, what their role and purpose will be, when they must be hired, and how the company plans to make

Figure I.2 The Plan stage of the Talent Acquisition Funnel

Figure I.3   The Prepare stage of the Talent Acquisition Funnel

such an acquisition. The human capital plan includes prioritizing your company's hiring needs in alignment with its resources (the three Cs).

PREPARE

The three key steps in the Prepare stage (see figure I.3) take the company-level human capital plan and help you set up the talent search for each role to be filled. This stage defines the role, its purpose, and the associated incentive design, and determines whether the process is going to be led internally or in partnership with a third-party recruiting firm. The combination of the Plan and Prepare stages will fundamentally change the outcome of your company's talent acquisition processes by attacking the challenge top-down.

EXECUTE

As the name suggests, the third stage is all about execution, where the company engages in the external due diligence of the market and candidates. Once your company gets through the first two stages, you are ready to start the process of finding candidates. The six steps of this stage (see figure I.4) are designed to increase your company's efficiency to systematically process a large pool of candidates and move them quickly through this stage of the funnel

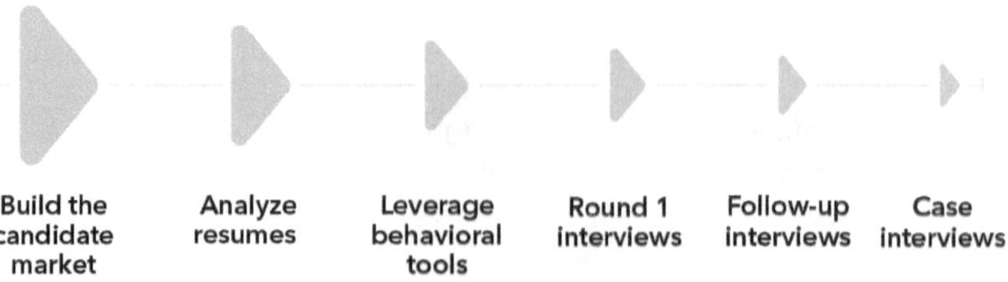

Figure I.4   The Execute stage of the Talent Acquisition Funnel

while maintaining the due diligence rigor necessary to find the best talent for the job.

One of the biggest pain points I hear from companies is the amount of time and energy wasted in reviewing dozens of bad resumes and interviewing unqualified candidates. By the time a good candidate surfaces, the hiring and acquiring team is often exhausted. The TAF solves this issue in two ways. First, early in the process, the funnel ensures the company can process a high volume of candidates using tools and processes to increase efficiency without compromising quality of diligence. Second, by being more efficient and thus spending less time per candidate earlier in the process, you and your teams can conserve your stamina to then be able to spend more time and focus on fewer preferred candidates in the back end of the process. This increases overall efficiency and effectiveness of your diligence. The outcome is a solid slate of thoroughly vetted candidates who have earned the right and your company's respect to be in the latter stages of the process.

This core of the TAF involves a thorough yet efficient due diligence approach with the intent of reaching the preferred candidate, with enough rigor, structure, and process that is repeatable and scalable for all roles and in any organization.

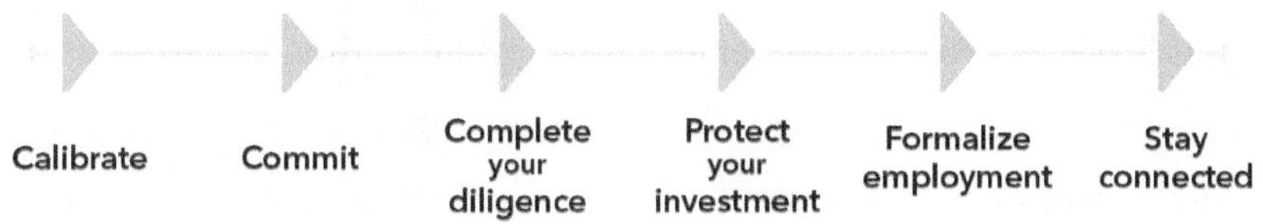

Figure I.5   The Close stage of the Talent Acquisition Funnel

CLOSE

The final stage of the TAF is to close on the winning candidate. I have seen far too many companies that get to this part of the process and, often because of exhaustion, simply rush through it and end up in a bad hiring situation. Those companies that systematically go through the six steps (see figure I.5) of this stage of the funnel tend to have much higher close rates but also a seamless crossboarding of the candidates.

I use the word *crossboarding* as opposed to *onboarding* because, contrary to common thinking where a company is the one who onboards a new employee (or when it acquires another company) to their culture, values, systems, and processes, the operational reality is that the employee is also onboarding the company to their ways of working, their principles and practices, and their values. Therefore, to call it *onboarding* only addresses half of what happens when a new employee joins your company.

This stage is a critical part of the diligence process where your company gets to choose the winner, continue your due diligence on that person by talking to their references and doing background checks, and ensure that the winning candidate continues to have an honest window into the company's values, practices, and processes.

This is also the most important stage for the talent, the human on the other side of all of this who is now considering your offer.

This is where the winning candidate, for the first time in the process, feels like they have earned the right to be able to sit at the table with enough credibility and leverage to have an understandably and deservedly selfish conversation. Up until this stage, the company is typically in the driver's seat, but now the winning candidate gets to have a strong position and a say about their needs as they relate to the role and terms of employment. Based on how you handle this stage of the funnel, the candidate is either going to feel even more excited about your company or discover that all the up-front "marketing" that they experienced was simply a cover. Remember, you may be hiring a lot of people, but the talent is only trying to get the one job that will give them the professional excitement they are seeking, help them take care of their families, and perhaps even inspire others around them to succeed.

The Close stage ensures sufficient external diligence on the winning candidate and a clear alignment on the terms of employment, making sure the candidate crosses the finish line having accepted the offer and excited to join your organization.

The four stages of the TAF provide a thorough top-down, due-diligence approach (akin to M&A) that ties your company's strategy and its people needs (see table I.1) with each stage and step, delivering outcomes that progressively inform your decisions.

The Benefits of the Talent Acquisition Funnel

The TAF is a simple, comprehensive, and rigorous method to meet the needs of CEOs, other business operators, and investors. Each of the four stages—Plan, Prepare, Execute, and Close—can be implemented in a modular way to help your company gradually build

Table I.1. Talent Acquisition Funnel outcomes

Stage	Step	Outcomes
Plan	Define strategy	Use a top-down approach to internal due diligence to drive clarity on *what* the company is solving for, by *when*, and *how* it will get there. This underpins the human capital plan that details *who* is needed, including specific skills and traits.
	Prioritize objectives	Understand the drivers of magnitude, volume, and velocity of change to ruthlessly prioritize initiatives, talent needs, and required levels of emotional intelligence (EQ) to execute change management.
	Align resources	Align resources (people, practice, and systems) to deliver on company talent acquisition priorities.
Prepare	Define the role	Clarify each role's deliverables (tied to top-down strategy) and requirements (experience, qualifications, leadership, and EQ traits).
	Design incentives	Design incentives to meet the role definition and deliverables, calibrated against internal budgets and market rates to compete successfully, and limit the need for recalibration later in the funnel.
	Determine your recruiting strategy	Establish company's internal capability and capacity to lead the recruiting efforts and determine whether it needs to partner with a third party to fill current gaps.
Execute	Build the candidate market	Identify specific market segments and channels to find candidates with the necessary requirements.
	Analyze resumes	Analyze key resume attributes to enable accelerated and early prioritization of preferred candidates.
	Leverage behavioral tools	Integrate automated tools to provide data andinsights and track your progress, to augment your TAF and optimize efficiency.
	Round 1 interviews	Validate resume content and pressure-test specific skills and traits. Explore technical and cultural fit for role requirements and diligence of candidate's intentions and motivations.
	Follow-up interviews	Give exposure to the broader team (distributing interview load and increasing exposure) to further pressure-test technical and cultural fit, as well as deep dive on EQ levels relative to requirements of the role.
	Case interviews	Use this practical diligence tool to assess a broad range of skills, including problem-solving, communication, and ability to handle pressure, giving candidates an opportunity to showcase their talent and understanding of the job.

continued →

Stage	Step	Outcomes
Close	Calibrate	Align on evaluation of case interview candidates to quickly reach a final decision on the winner.
	Commit	Make an offer. Act quickly to secure your preferred candidate, and ensure alignment between company budget, candidate's needs, and market rates.
	Complete your diligence	Conduct thoughtful reference checks to deepen your knowledge of the candidate and inform how to work with, develop, and get the most out of candidates.
	Protect your investment	Use background checks to ensure no legal issues and liabilities associated with the winning candidate.
	Formalize employment	Complete contractual memorialization (via email, letter, or agreement) of the employment terms, including incentive plans, performance reviews, and cadence of check-ins to avoid future misalignments.
	Stay connected	Continue communicating to ensure that the offeree is engaged and, most importantly, shows up to work on their first day.

its foundation for distinctive talent acquisition capabilities while ensuring alignment with the company's vision and values. Each stage of the funnel and the steps within each stage builds on the previous one, creating a streamlined approach that systematically solves the challenges that CEOs, business owners, and investors frequently face during talent acquisition.

The TAF is designed to be simple to make it easier to implement, adopt, own, tweak, and scale to your own needs as well as the needs of the business. In addition to ease of implementation, other key benefits include thoroughness of due diligence, creation of capability and capacity within your business, and prioritization of associated capital.

What's truly exciting is that with the availability of artificial intelligence (AI) tools, businesses can now amplify the velocity and efficiency with which they execute the strategies and operational steps of the TAF. AI tools can complement the implementation of the TAF, serving as powerful enablers that accelerate adoption and execution of your talent acquisition goals.

EASE OF IMPLEMENTATION

The simplicity of the TAF makes it easy for your company to implement it both operationally and culturally. While I strongly recommend implementing the entire TAF as described in the rest of this book, I have designed the funnel to be modular so organizations can add any of the four stages into their existing processes. Similarly, for those companies with a thorough talent acquisition process, it is possible to carefully insert select TAF steps to increase the efficiency and yield of their existing process without having to upend it entirely. Finally, companies that don't intend to change their process sequence or steps and yet want to improve their overall acquisition engine can simply leverage the principles and practices that I share in this book. The flexibility of this methodology, its tools, principles, and practices offer a range of implementation choices for companies looking to improve their in-house ability to consistently acquire top talent.

THOROUGHNESS OF DUE DILIGENCE

The TAF offers a level of due diligence that is commensurate with the importance of your company's most valuable asset: its people. Acquiring the best and the brightest while ferociously competing in a tough talent supply market commands this level of thoroughness. When a company wants to acquire other businesses, it builds internal M&A capabilities, leverages its capacity and invests capital to do a thorough diligence on the target, and ensures that the right market price is paid to acquire the asset. Similarly, each stage and step of the

TAF offers key insights into the capabilities of the candidates relative to the strategic needs of the company and requirements of the role, allowing you to be as well informed as possible as you filter candidates through the funnel.

CREATING CAPABILITY WITHIN THE BUSINESS

The TAF creates capability to acquire talent agnostic of the scale or type of business. This happens in a few different ways. First and foremost is the mindset and intention with which the company approaches talent acquisition. While the need to hire people may be obvious, the TAF gives your company the ability and opportunity to think about your talent requirements in a top-down process that is principally grounded in the company's strategic plans. This method also forces you to systematically think about what you are trying to solve for and how new talent is going to help get you there. Additionally, the principles of how to run a thorough yet high-paced diligence process, while also being mindful of how to respectfully engage with candidates, helps improve your competitive advantage in talent acquisition.

Second, capability building comes from the *process*. The TAF offers a structured, modular, repeatable, and scalable process. The specific sequence of steps, key KPIs, and data required to meet threshold values along the funnel increases your company's ability to have a thorough candidate evaluation process. Having a simple, practical, and structured approach that is reliable and repeatable allows you to filter candidates systematically and consistently through the funnel and at a competitive cadence. Also, the TAF forces your company (and its management and investors) to evaluate the volume and velocity of hiring to align with the company's capability, giving you an opportunity to genuinely consider the need for third-party help when necessary.

A third contributor to your company's talent acquisition capability has to do with the TAF's systematic use of process and behavioral tools. The practice and principle of using tools is way more important than the use of any one specific tool. The TAF can work with tools ranging from those developed in-house to licensed third-party technology. Whether these tools help you manage sequencing and timing of each of the process steps, capture candidate-specific data, codify feedback from everyone involved in the process, or track applicants through the funnel, the net benefit is to create capacity and efficiency in your TAF to close on candidates quickly. Data from these tools augments the quality of your diligence early in the process and increases your company's capability to run candidates through the funnel at a higher cadence, which helps compete in a highly fluid and competitive talent market.

Finally, the TAF helps your company better use its *people* to find and attract talent. The funnel is grounded in team-led diligence as opposed to a one-person process. This allows the company to benefit from the collective experience of the organization. It also builds in-house capability around such teamwork and avoids bottlenecks and biases that can arise with only one or two people leading the recruiting processes, as is common in many organizations. The other benefits of team engagement are improved transparency on a critical business process and a healthier company culture.

CREATING CAPACITY INSIDE THE BUSINESS

The TAF increases capacity (time and mindshare) within your company by improving both the efficiency and the effectiveness of its recruiting process. First, the funnel reduces the amount of wasted time. Part of this happens from the improved capability highlighted above. Having a human capital plan aligned with the top-down strategy minimizes the time sink often driven by constant internal debates and iterations during the acquisition process. These process iterations and sunk time get even more pronounced when your company needs to hire either senior folks (high magnitude of change) or many people (high volume). Associated with the top-down prioritization and planning, the TAF allows alignment with market-based pricing to further avoid the wasted time and effort that arises from major misalignment of a candidate's expectations with the company's budget, which can eventually lead to an offer being rejected, forcing the company to go back to the drawing board.

Second, the source of capacity creation comes from increasing the available time to assess and hire top talent. The TAF does this by relying on a team rather than one or two individuals, which increases both the collective available capacity of your company and the velocity of the process. It leads to quicker decision-making, allowing the company to close faster on candidates and minimize the risk of losing them to competition. Additionally, the Talent Acquisition Funnel's use of data to eliminate weaker candidates earlier and quicker increases team capacity by saving time that would otherwise be lost interviewing those candidates. Finally, leveraging the TAF's principles and framework to decide whether to outsource market building and project management work to third-party recruiting firms (where necessary and possible) helps further save a portion of your team's capacity.

One of the major benefits of the TAF is that your company can reduce its time investment per candidate during the earlier stages of recruitment. This allows more time for better-quality interactions with

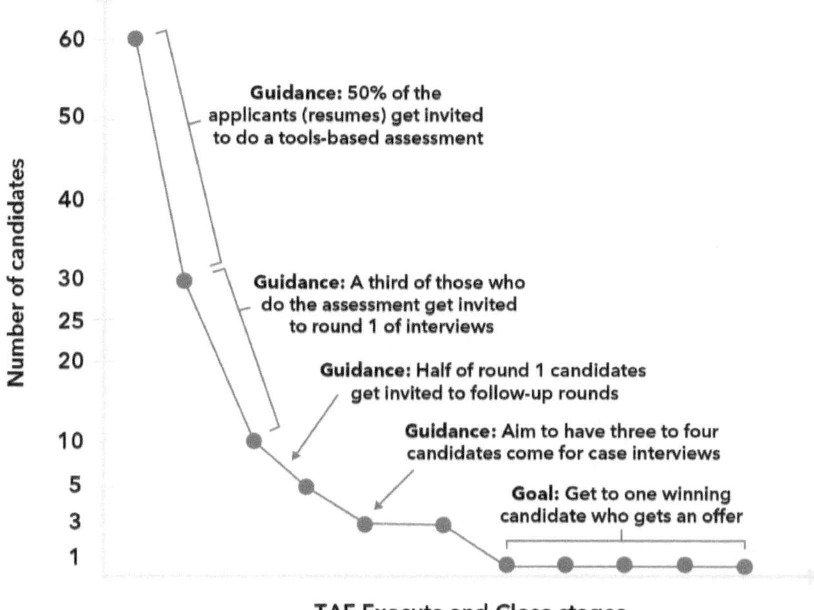

Figure I.6 The Talent Acquisition Funnel candidate yield curve

fewer candidates in later stages. Figure I.6 shows this acceleration through the funnel and the typical TAF pass-through rates at each step.

With a focus of less time per candidate in the front end of the funnel, the TAF creates capacity for management to be able to spend more quality time with fewer candidates in the back end of the funnel.

PLAN

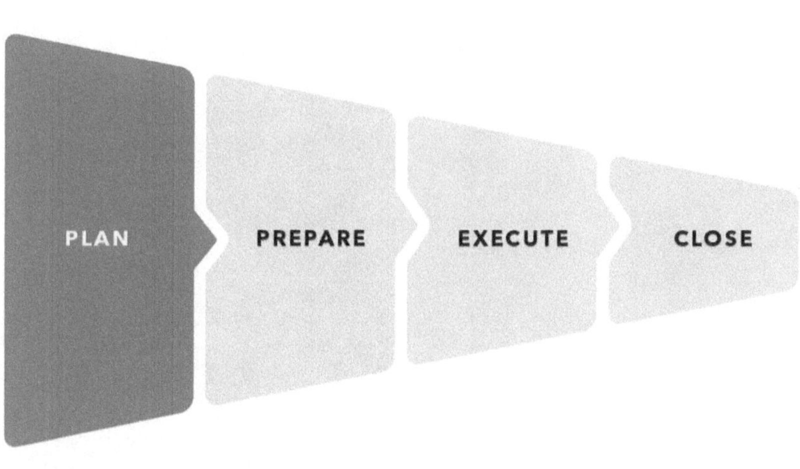

CHAPTER 1

DEFINE STRATEGY

We are a high-growth company with the incredible
mission to help millions of people reverse diabetes. Without
a long-term growth strategy supported by a twelve-month
tactical plan based on strategic prioritization, I would not
even know where to begin my human capital or talent plan
to help me with why to hire, who to hire, when to hire.

—**AMIT SHAH**, COO of Virta Health, USA[1]

TALENT ACQUISITION IS MOST SUCCESSFUL when the company first has a clear growth strategy for the short and medium terms, followed by a clear, top-down human capital strategy. Companies whose human capital needs are directly derived from their growth strategy tend to acquire talent that creates the highest gains in enterprise value. Conceptually, it's quite simple: The human capital plan is at the core of *how* you are going to execute your overall strategy that focuses on what you are solving for, what you are trying to achieve, why are you trying to achieve these goals, and when you plan to execute the initiatives and expect to experience their benefits.

CEOs often ask me the level of detail they need to have in their strategic plans to be able to extract or develop their human capital plan. The idea is not to have a management-consulting-style detailed sixty-page PowerPoint document. Simply having more content pages does not mean you have a better plan or strategy, but what matters more is that you have clear, thoughtful, and high-quality (not quantity) goals that galvanize the organization.

In the world where most CEOs are time poor, the output of this strategy work can be a few simple pages that summarize the tenets of *what, when, how,* and *who.* The *what* is what the company is solving for when it comes to growth, from the point of view of both qualitative deliverables (the quality of service, customer satisfaction, company culture goals, etc.) and quantitative deliverables (such as revenue, gross margin, net profit, and EBITDA targets). *When* is a breakdown of the *what* according to a discrete timeline ranging from a monthly to a quarterly work plan. For a longer (multiyear) range strategy, annual goals will make sense. *How* is a list of prioritized operational initiatives that deliver against the *what* and *when.* For the *who,* each initiative will need an owner who will lead the effort and who will be accountable for the project.

I encourage any company that wishes to build a medium-term outlook that goes beyond twelve months to build a plan no longer than three years out. For such plans, it is best to stick to broad-strokes objectives across the same buckets mentioned above. The difference is that the level of precision will understandably be much lower. For example, your *what* may just be a range for revenues or EBITDA, your *when* might simply be the first or second half of the year or at best quarters, and the *how* and the *who* might be very high-level initiatives with the names or titles of select executive sponsors against each. Although this medium-term plan will be less precise than your twelve-month plan, it is still important to break down this medium-term strategic work across the categories of *what*, *when*, *how*, and *who*.

My practice and a strong recommendation is to start with a tactical twelve-month strategy and work plan, which eventually translates into the annual budget, as well as a top-down three-year view focused on annual deliverables rather than monthly or quarterly outcomes.

On the topic of talent acquisition, the next step is bottom-up, where the owner (who) of each initiative should build a comprehensive project plan, including a resource plan highlighting the staffing needs of all the new strategic projects and to support the day-to-day work to run the existing business. The aggregation of these plans is the critical input into the company's human capital strategy and planning. This way, the people needs, for both the growth and the maintenance of the business, create the human capital plan for the company. Figure 1.1 captures the structural breakdown of the drivers of human capital demand that inform the company's human capital plan.

Day-to-day reactive needs arise from either a voluntary resignation from an employee or an unplanned involuntary termination of employment. In such situations, you know the type of person you need, as you have hired for that position before.

Growth-related reactive needs arise when a company faces a sudden increase in resource needs from an unplanned increase in demand. For example, a customer may suddenly decide to give you more work; perhaps they want to consolidate vendors or have had a growth spurt. Or there may be a shift in the macro climate, such as a change in a business's regulatory or compliance needs, requiring you to quickly hire resources to match the needs from this sudden change.

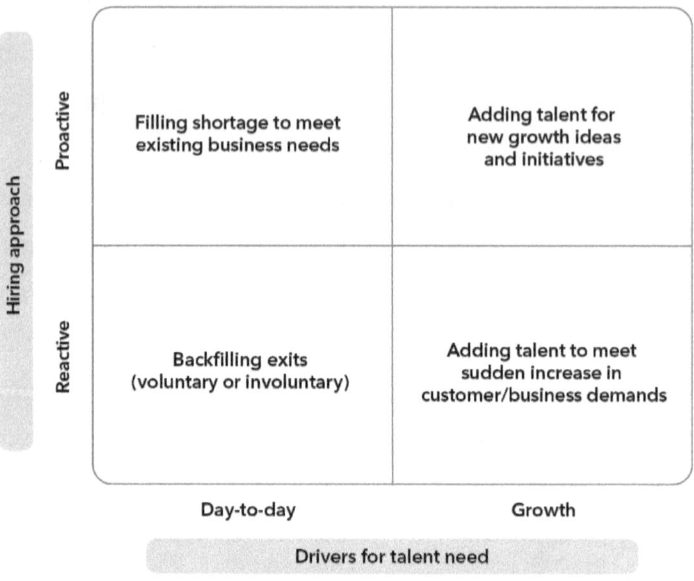

Figure 1.1 Drivers of human capital demand

Day-to-day proactive needs are when you strategically and, therefore, intentionally want to hire more people to meet the existing business needs. These are often captured in your open and unfilled positions to meet current staff shortages.

Growth-related proactive needs also tie back to your company's growth strategy, such as planning to launch a new service or product or entering a new market needing the resources who can do that work. With a proactive search, a company will be able to take the time to do thorough due diligence to understand the type of talent it needs, the current market conditions for talent supply and demand, and the time and capital needed to acquire such folks.

The key tenets of the human capital plan include overall organizational design; the timing and sequencing of hiring; the roles and responsibilities for each hire; titles, reporting structure, and compensation, including incentive levels for each position; and the performance metrics associated with each role. To develop the company's overall organizational strategy and design, CEOs, executive management, and investors should outline the changes in organizational design that will take place because of all the proactive hiring both for the growth strategy and for day-to-day operational needs. Mapping out the new talent's placement within the organization allows your company and its investors (where relevant) to get a sense of the various leverage points each new hire will bring to the company. Additionally, this exercise allows your management team to visualize the organizational design of the company before and after all the planned changes. Companies have found this exercise to be incredibly informative and sometimes humbling (depending on the level of change). It allows them to take a step back and reflect on the aggregate levels of change they are trying to bring into the business and gives them an opportunity to determine if and how they will be able to successfully implement all the changes.

As Vance Chang, CFO at Dine Brands Global (NYSE: DIN), owner of Applebee's and IHOP, shared with me:

Teams must be built for the long haul. Talent, even the best ones, need time to settle in and develop. When I look to bring a new talent onto our team, I need to be clear not just on the track record and experience but also on the full buy-in on what we are trying to build. Driving growth and creating value in a sustainable way takes time and may not happen in a straight line. Sometimes I want to shake things up too. It is critical for me to have clarity around how each individual aligns with our long-term plans for the company and the team.[2]

Regarding the timing of a new hire, your company can better execute when it is able to clearly articulate the timing and sequencing of all the proactive hiring, tying it back to the financial and operational outcomes it has budgeted for in the next twelve months. To accommodate the imprecision of timing the talent availability in the market, it is helpful to start with a quarterly view on your timing of hire. In other words, knowing the quarter you would like to have someone starting in their role is probably as precise as you can get in today's hiring market. Finally, a thoughtful organizational design should also clarify reporting lines and accountability structure across the organizational stack. This creates a level of clarity and transparency with significant cultural benefits in a growing company. To illustrate this, let me walk you through an example of a US-based B2B services business I was recently working with.

First came the growth strategy (*what*, *when*, and *how*): I joined their multiday cross-functional annual strategy offsite with the CEO and the executive leadership team. We first developed the company's short- and medium-term strategic plans and then designed operational initiatives to achieve those goals. The company decided that, in the next twelve months (*when*), it would like to achieve a 20 percent increase in gross revenue over the previous fiscal year's (*what*). With this growth target and timeline in mind, the management identified three initiatives (two new and one existing) that would help them achieve this goal. This was their *how*.

Then came the human capital (*who*) strategy: From the growth strategy, the company determined its human (and financial) capital needs to implement each of these initiatives. According to figure 1.1, the company sat in the top-right quadrant: That is, it needed to proactively acquire talent for growth initiatives. An assessment was made to bring four new people on the team to help reach the target.

For the organizational design, two of the four people would be added to the account management function (which also served as inside sales) that was part of operations and eventually reported to the COO. One person would join the technical development team, which reported to the CTO. The fourth person was a senior salesperson who would lead the launch of a new market for the company. Given the importance of this initiative, this new salesperson would report to the CEO for the first twelve months. Afterward, if the initiative was going as planned (or better) the person would then start reporting to the COO, who oversaw many of the company's other sales-related activities.

Given the company's goal of year-over-year actualized growth of 20 percent, they needed to book the new gross revenue by the end of the year. The new salesperson was going to account for 50 percent of the 20 percent total targeted growth. Working backward, this meant the company needed to have someone in place by the end of first quarter of the fiscal year to allow the new salesperson to have enough time to get crossboarded, to become familiar with the company culture and its service offering, and to leverage their personal network to sell. Given the criticality of this role to the company's strategic and financial objectives and the importance of the technical developer role, the company prioritized talent acquisition efforts with those two roles and decided to postpone the search for two account managers.

For the salesperson, the role, responsibilities, and compensation had precedence and did not need to be reinvented but tweaked slightly to accommodate the strategy of entering a new market segment for the company. To reflect that, specific attributes to the role description (and therefore the job description) were added. Finally, compensation was structured such that a large percentage of the salesperson's income was tied to revenue booked by the company from the new market. Additionally, KPIs around the customer acquisition funnel, lead generation data, extent of CRM data completion, and some qualitative performance metrics were included in the overall incentive structure for the employee. By starting top-down and consciously prioritizing a key growth initiative, the company was able to focus on an extremely time-sensitive talent requirement and identify specific experience and performance attributes required in the new role. This clarity and sense of urgency allowed them to enter the market with ample time to complete a thorough search process, ultimately finding the right salesperson who was able to hit the ground running.

This example is a simplified real-life case study that highlights the connectivity of a company's top-down growth strategy with its human capital strategy. Clarifying what it is trying to achieve and the type, quality, and timing of talent acquisition to get there is the best way to ensure success.

KEY TAKEAWAYS

✓ What are you solving for? Clarity on the strategic and operational goals (the *why* and the *what*) of the company allows management to figure out the *when* and the *how* and ultimately the *who*.

✓ A major part of delivering against the goals and vision of the company is to have a human capital plan that is tied to its growth strategy—the right people in the right seats at the right times with the right purpose.

✓ Reactive hiring that arises from people quitting, when put through the lens of priority of needs, can help manage the hiring pressures. Similarly, proactive hiring through the same lens can create the required sense of urgency around talent acquisition.

CHAPTER 2

PRIORITIZE OBJECTIVES

As **CEOS AND OPERATORS,** we often feel we have an endless list of to-dos, from tactical day-to-day planned and unplanned projects to large strategic initiatives. All of them seem important and require our attention and company's resources. To add to the challenge of the varying *magnitudes* of these projects, the sheer *volume* of work can put significant strain on a company's resources. And to top it all off, the company needs to get things done with a certain *velocity*. Whether a customer needs immediate attention or you have chosen a project to finish by an aggressive timeline, the speed of implementation also creates pressure on existing company resources, particularly its biggest resource: its people. To manage the combined effect of magnitude, volume, and velocity on your company's ability to implement change, prioritizing becomes crucial.

Building your teams by acquiring talent is a major change project in itself. There is a duality to this change. First, the addition of new talented employees will create change in your company's structure and culture. Then there is change that is introduced from the work they end up leading and delivering. Given the combined impact, talent acquisition requires its own prioritization discipline.

The company needs to start with a top-down company-level assessment to identify what elements of their strategy and growth plans are the highest priority and, therefore, what new roles they need to prioritize to deliver those critical goals. At the same time, a balance must be maintained between the capital available to hire such roles and the organization's ability to absorb new talent. Overlaying that with when the new employees should be on the team to achieve timely growth and change management objectives for the company is also part of the initial prioritization. Ruthless prioritization of your strategic objectives will help you proactively avoid the trap of taking on too many major change projects with too little time. This prevents enormous burden on the company's resources that can lead to failed outcomes, burnout, and often loss of great talent.

Then the company must prioritize, at the individual talent level, the top-priority skills and traits critical to the success of the role and to achieve the company's strategic growth objectives. The company needs to identify not only top-priority technical skills required from their future employee but also leadership, cultural, and emotional intelligence (EQ) elements necessary for them to be successful in the role and at the company.

The Magnitude of Change

While big-change projects can have a massive impact on the business, they also suck up a lot of resources and require gestation time for the company and its people to absorb the changes. Most CEOs and

DEMAND FOR EMOTIONAL INTELLIGENCE (EQ)

As part of the prioritization process, it is inevitable for you to think about how the new hire will implement major change initiatives. Most CEOs tell me that for their businesses to reach peak performance, they need more than intellectual and technical horsepower in their leadership team. The key ingredient the majority of CEOs highlight is emotional intelligence (EQ). My simplistic operational definition of EQ is people skills. It is often synonymous with traits such as empathy, listening skills, self-awareness, and soft skills. Leaders with high EQ are known to be able to help their companies successfully and consistently navigate transformational changes to accelerate growth, making EQ a major topic that is top of mind for leaders around the world. This is why when defining the key requirements of the role, identifying and prioritizing the required levels of EQ from your new hire is critical. A new leader with the right levels of EQ will help you effect planned changes in your organization and also allow them to be successful in their role.

As David Brown, a UK-based mental performance and leadership expert who is a mentor to elite global champions in Formula 1, soccer, and golf, as well as global executives, explained:

> Personal peak performance requires the minimization of interferences. For a team to be high performing requires deep trust and the ability to have challenging conversations. Each of these conditions can only be met with a high EQ baseline.[1]

There are three key situations in an organization that can affect the EQ needs in a role and hence affect your hiring prioritization.

continued →

BUSINESS CONTEXT

A current or desired situation in the business can drive high-EQ needs. For instance, high employee turnover or attrition; high volume of M&A; transitioning founders or leadership team; strategic desire for cultural changes; rapid scaling of the business; remote team management; or right-sizing of the organization are all situations that require leaders to have significant people skills.

BUSINESS MODEL AND STRATEGY

Businesses with a high-touch model such as a B2B services business, health care, education, or hospitality will require high-EQ professionals to deliver a service that is thoughtful and empathetic. But not all industries and customers need or value a white glove service. In such cases you may be able to toggle the levels of EQ needed in your employees.

BUSINESS MISSION AND VALUES

Your mission both requires and attracts high-EQ talent. Both non-profit organizations (charities, hospitals, educational organizations, environmental entities) and for-profit companies (senior care, mental health clinics, consumer finance) may want higher-EQ team members. Similarly, companies wanting to live their values such as respect, integrity, empathy, and teamwork will want to acquire talent that exhibits such traits.

investors inherently know that the cumulative magnitude of change that a company and its management can handle is often a lot less than what most teams ambitiously put on paper. Yet, when I walk through the annual plan or strategic review with a company's management, many times I find that they wish to complete roughly half a dozen major transformational change management projects in the next twelve months. While I love the ambition and aspiration, that magnitude of change is simply not practical for most businesses to execute and absorb in such a short window.

On top of new projects, there are always a half a dozen or more ongoing projects. Then to add to the proactive projects either in play or those being proposed, every company is bound to face a barrage of reactive smaller projects that are going to drive incremental changes in the business.

As CEOs, operators, and investors, it is our job to be the change leaders and managers by thinking of projects that will fundamentally change our business. However, the reality is that a company and its people can only absorb so much change at a time. A single big project can absorb a company's major resources during execution, and the employees may need a significant amount of time to digest those changes. All of this leads to an inevitably heavy strain on management's ability to effect and measure impact at the individual project level when there is so much change happening simultaneously. The hard part is being able to prioritize a few projects that you can execute successfully while letting go of others. Therefore, my tactical counsel to companies is to ruthlessly prioritize your projects starting by separating the magnitude of each one into three categories.

First come the *transformational* projects that can fundamentally change your business. Your company should take on no more than two of these in one year for the reasons mentioned above. Typical examples of these transformational projects include selling your business, M&A, implementing a new technology solution such as NetSuite or Salesforce, launching a new product or service, changing your business model, or expanding into a new territory. In the case of talent acquisition, transformational change can come from finding a new CEO as your successor, hiring your direct reports, or reshaping your entire organizational structure.

Then there are *substantial* projects that may not be transformative but still have a major impact on your business. Your company can successfully navigate three to four of these projects in one year with the scale and scope dictating whether you need more or fewer. These projects include changing your pricing structure, redefining roles and responsibilities, and changing the incentive plans for your people. As it relates to talent acquisition, this could include hiring middle management, recalibrating titles, and changing compensation structures such as bonuses and commissions.

Finally, smaller, *incremental* projects pop up throughout the year that are both reactive and proactive. I tend to have no hard rules on how many of these you can strategize for, because most of them are about blocking and tackling the day-to-day of any operations.

A simple organizational structure can be used for categorizing your human capital. Here, level 1 is you, the CEO; level 2 are the direct reports to the CEO; level 3s report to level 2s; and so on (see figure 2.1). This nomenclature works well for businesses whose relative organizational size is small so that the organizational structure is kept simple.

Depending on the seniority of the role you are trying to fill, it could have multiple levels of change and impact. For the example of finding your direct report (level 2), be it a functional head or someone leading a business unit, the initial impact is on you to handle this transformational project. This senior person's introduction to the company will be a catalyst for major change the organization has to absorb. Additionally, the deliverables from their work will also have

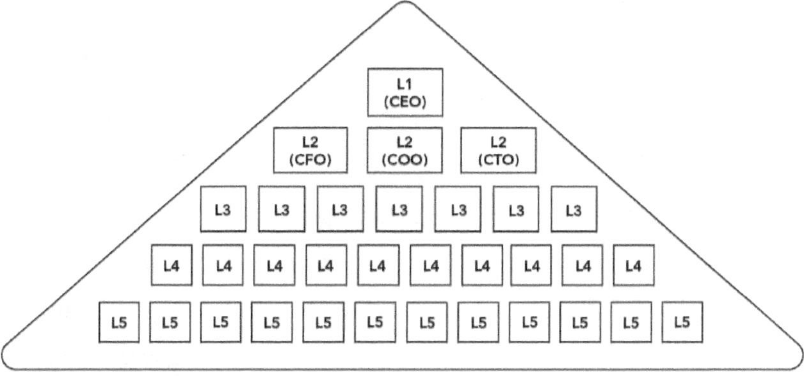

Figure 2.1 Organizational structure in a private business

significant change in the company's operations. This cumulatively creates a significant transformational change for the company.

If, on the other hand, you are trying to hire someone more tactical (e.g., a field or production worker), then the magnitude of change on the overall organization will generally be low. This is because such candidates may not have the decision rights to have transformational influence on the business but also because they are likely joining a much larger preexisting pool of peers where the impact of one person gets diluted.

Companies who handle this well tend to strategically acquire only one or two level 2 people at a time. They give these hires, as well as the rest of the organization, an opportunity to assimilate before embarking on the next big hire. This, of course, precludes the situation where you need to make multiple executive and mid-level organizational changes in the company. In those instances, the best practice is to acknowledge the magnitude of change to which you are exposing the company, identify the risks associated with such changes, and then manage those risks.

Jorge Gross, Managing Partner at US private equity firm Trivest Partners, put it well:

> As an investor, I intellectually want to get as much done as I possibly can to increase the enterprise value of my portfolio companies. But when it comes to people, I need to be very clinical about who I bring in, how many big changes I can make, and how the team will gel together to accelerate value creation. If not done thoughtfully, I know from experience a business can lose a lot of value—and people—very quickly.[2]

The Volume of Change

Hiring too many people simultaneously and across all levels is risky for most organizations, as it quickly taxes the company's capability, capacity, and capital. For example, if the investors or the board decide to hire a new CEO as well as multiple level 2 and level 3 employees, then the sheer volume of hires is impossible for most (if not all) organizations to digest, not to mention it becomes difficult to extract the enterprise value impact underwritten in those hires and in the preferred timeline. Then there are instances—such as when a company wins a major new project, a client decides to increase the volume of projects with the company, or the company is in high growth mode—when the workload can immediately increase, which leads to the need for a high volume of hiring. Similarly, if a few senior folks leave in quick succession, the company will need to acquire senior talent to replace them, both to infuse leadership and to stabilize the existing staff to minimize attrition.

When the volume of change becomes too much to handle, its execution becomes difficult. Simply put, you just can't do it all. When the volume of hiring gets really high, without an infusion of additional recruiting capability and capacity, most companies struggle to hire all the people they need while maintaining quality and speed.

Crossboarding becomes difficult when you hire several level 2 and 3 employees simultaneously. Too many new hires all at once can also create cultural issues. The new senior team, having not worked together previously and being new to the organization, need the runway to settle in and understand their job; to understand the incumbent culture while also figuring out which changes they can influence, and if or how they can do so; and to get to know their new peers, who may have also recently joined and are in the same discovery boat as them.

The other impact of high-volume hiring, particularly at the executive level but even in the middle-management ranks, is that it becomes difficult for incumbent employees to adjust to new leadership styles, approaches, and expectations. In some cases, employees can even become uncomfortable enough with so much change that they quit.

Finally, customer issues emerge when too many new people, particularly in customer-facing roles, end up confusing customers who are used to your existing people, structure, and services. This can not only cause customer dissatisfaction but also lead to loss of customers and revenue.

Companies who are successful in hiring a high volume of people have a more measured, top-down systematic approach. For instance, if they need a CEO, they first apply all their capability and capacity and a necessary amount of capital to get that done. Knowing that this person is going to shape the future of the company and its people, they avoid hiring the next layers of the organization until this individual has had an opportunity to settle in and is able to develop their own growth strategy and human capital plan. They apply this to all major leadership roles.

This space gives the new leader an opportunity to shape their own organization. It is the right and respectful thing to do, as it shows them your sincerity and commitment in allowing the leader to have decision rights and to have an impact on the company. It provides them with the runway to understand the incumbent culture, a chance to determine the changes they wish to make, and the timeline in which they wish to execute. They can then acquire talent that fits with their style, needs, values, and cultural goals for the company. This has a positive flow-on effect, as the future hires get an opportunity to get to know their boss through the interview and diligence process, allowing them to make an informed choice on mutual fit.

Additionally, companies that are successful with high-volume hiring assess all the major risks—cultural, financial, and operational—associated with hiring many people in proximity and develop an implementation plan that mitigates those risks. These plans include who will be hired and when, tie back to the strategic plan, indicate ownership by talent acquisition champions (whoever in the company will take point for individual or collective hiring), and include a cadence of internal project reviews to ensure support and accountability for those who are leading the acquisition efforts.

Next, those companies that measure the impact, both quantitative and qualitative, of multiple new hires tend to better navigate the process of high-volume hiring. Being systematic allows companies to measure and track key metrics regarding the effects of high-volume hiring on their people, customers, and culture. Some such metrics include employee and customer retention data, job and customer satisfaction levels, appropriate speed of high-volume acquisitions, and employee morale. Changes to the culture, both proactive and reactive, should be assessed, with 360° feedback tools or one-on-one discussions with employees.

As Pam Vona, CEO and Cofounder of the US-based Center for Safe and Resilient Schools and Workplaces, stated:

When I interview someone, my top priority isn't technical prowess—my team can handle and assess that thoroughly. As CEO, I focus on assessing maturity, empathy, collaboration, and cultural alignment with the team. I want to ensure that anyone joining us can handle emotional challenges and be a constructive teammate. Ultimately, I am trying to assess whether this person will become a trusted member of the team. Without these traits, there is risk that this new hire may damage team dynamics, erode psychological safety, and quietly undo the very culture you are working to build and maintain.[3]

The moral of the story is not that a company should not or cannot hire a lot of people. But for a company to be able to tackle high-volume hiring, it needs to strengthen its talent acquisition capability and capacity. To do so, it needs to have an intentional, systematic, top-down implementation process (capability) whose impact can be measured and tracked. Having the right people—such as a talent acquisition champion—focusing on this task adds the capacity required to get high-volume recruiting done successfully.

One such example involves a US-based web development company. They wanted to hire five developers and two project managers to help support several large projects they had recently won. Up until this point, the company had only ever hired three people simultaneously into the company. Furthermore, this was often with the benefit of foresight due to voluntary exits and employees giving periods of notice. The CEO was the de facto talent acquisition champion, who somehow managed to fit the hiring into his day job. But now, the company had to grow by nearly 50 percent in less than six weeks. There was no way for the CEO to handle this volume at this velocity. To solve the problem, they decided to have the Head of Operations become the talent acquisition champion and also hired a contingent recruiter to help with execution. This strategy allowed the CEO to be involved in the key parts of the interview process while not feeling like they were spread too thin. Also, leveraging the Head of Operations allowed the CEO to use that capacity for making the hiring decisions, negotiating the offers, and successfully filling the seven roles before the project kicked off.

The Velocity of Change

As operators, we seldom feel like time is on our side. Our customers want answers yesterday, our employees need attention today, and our vendors don't always respond quickly enough. Whatever the scenario, finding the right balance between getting projects done on time and having enough time can sometimes feel like a beautiful dream. And when it comes to acquiring talent, we can often feel like we don't hire the right people quickly enough.

While it is important to be efficient in your talent acquisition process, companies that rush to make hiring decisions at the expense of thorough due diligence tend to consistently find downstream issues with their new hires and often get caught in an unproductive and never-ending hiring cycle. Those organizations that lean toward quality of diligence while ensuring high process efficiency tend to generate the highest benefits for themselves and their new hires. Pacing yourself in the talent acquisition journey can lead to several benefits.

First, not rushing through the process gives you the best opportunity to use your capability more effectively. In a world of limited resources, talent acquisition commands the skills and experience of the same group of people who also run the day-to-day of the business. Allowing an appropriate amount of runway for the process to unfold increases your chances of success. Rushing the decision-makers during the diligence stage can lead to missed data points and the wrong hiring decisions.

Second, allowing a longer runway for the due diligence process will also give you the opportunity to use your team's capacity efficiently by accommodating any preexisting constraints within the hiring team.

Finally, pacing yourself gives you the opportunity to adjust with the market. None of us can control the market and the associated supply-and-demand characteristics. By taking the appropriate time to run a search, your company can calibrate or pivot as necessary by paying attention to the market forces and listening to the feedback from third parties (assuming you have asked them to partner with your company) such as recruiting firms, who are most well informed on the market dynamics.

At a measured pace you can perform thorough diligence. When it comes to building the strongest muscle of your company—your people—there should be no shortcuts. Taking the time to understand your needs, the market conditions, and each of the candidates as they go through the funnel is the only way to find the right person who is both technically qualified to do the job and likely to be a great culture fit in your company.

And remember: *High velocity* does not always mean *high efficiency*. The truth is that if you move with high speed, you may achieve the numerical outcome of filling a position. However, if it turns out that the new hire's technical and cultural fits are overestimated during the diligence process, then the company will need to go back to the drawing board. Restarting the search and the entire journey all over again will be much slower the second time around, as the market of candidates goes a bit cold and reenergizing the talent pool takes much longer. Then there is the reputational or PR damage resulting from the company's haste. In the grand scheme of things, the *total* time the company ends up taking to fill the role is much higher, making them less efficient. The moral of the story from companies that successfully apply this concept is to take your time to do it right the first time.

One cautionary tale of high velocity involves a privately held real estate services company based out of Chicago with over eighty staff, nearly $12 million in annual revenues, and 15 percent EBITDA, who had done a great job recognizing the need for a senior operations person. The CEO and founder of the business is an incredibly resourceful and charismatic person who had a strong network in the region. Once the role was identified, he quickly spread the word through text messages, emails, and calls that he was hiring. Soon, referrals started coming in, and before he knew it, he was meeting with candidates. Within two weeks, he had met with over a dozen people. He ended up doing a handshake deal with one person after meeting them twice, once over coffee and once at dinner. With good intentions, he announced the hire to his entire staff, who were all caught by surprise, and notified his top three customers that he had made a significant hire. However, two weeks later, on their first day, the employee never showed up and did not answer any phone calls, text messages, or emails. Three days after that, the CEO finally got an email from the candidate. They had decided to stay at their current company, as their current boss had offered higher pay and a better title. The CEO, naturally fuming, felt humiliated to have to let his employees and customers know this had happened. Sadly, the other candidates who did not get the offer now knew they were not the CEO's top choice. Many decided to withdraw their candidacy, which led to relaunching the search, and because of poor market interest, filling the role took increasingly long, and the CEO had to explain the backstory to future candidates. The bottom line is that it was an incredible mess. While the CEO was eventually able to find the right person, what should have taken less than ninety days took nearly six months, with not only a reputational hit but also a loss in productivity and enterprise value.

High-velocity hiring is not always avoidable, however, because of both reactive and proactive needs. For example, when key folks, such as an operations manager, marketing lead, or salesperson, quit in proximity to one another and without much notice, a company has no choice but to react with speed to avoid chaos in the organization and the loss of business.

When I was involved with ValleyCrest operations, we needed to quickly hire a high volume of seasonal field employees every year. The key for successful hiring at high velocity was for us to build capability through process and apply it consistently when the need arose. Also, if you need to hire at high speed, you need to be able to create capacity in the system to manage that and avoid a major mistake many companies make (and I have made my share of these): a knee-jerk hiring decision, which almost always leads to a bad hire. To accommodate this annual hiring spree, we did two things. First, we built a consistent playbook that benefited from experiences of all the seasoned operators in the company having dealt with this in previous years. Second, all the GMs and local managers proactively created capacity in their weeks leading up to this recruitment drive to ensure they were dedicating significant time and energy to ensure effective and high-velocity hiring. Because we planned for it, we were able to quickly staff a large percentage of our field teams every year.

Similarly, when a senior salesperson quit at one of my portfolio companies, we knew that to find someone quickly, we needed to create capacity within our executive management team (in this case, the COO) to focus on this project. We assessed the portfolio of projects on their plate and decided what needed to pause to allow them to dedicate time and mindshare to focus on this unannounced but necessary high-speed project. Applying this dedicated capacity was one of the primary reasons we were able to hire someone from the industry within eight weeks and managed to avoid minimal loss of annual sales runway for the company.

Effectiveness is key in the hiring process, even over the necessary speed. Good things take time, and in the case of talent acquisition, time is needed for the company to run their process and find the right person. Focusing on quality over speed will help your company stay calm when the process goes on longer than you'd hoped.

By giving yourself the appropriate time to run a thorough talent acquisition process, you can manage one of the biggest drivers of risk: change. The more quickly you add people to your ecosystem, the higher the likelihood of cultural imbalance. By taking the time to run your process, you also allow those involved, such as the hiring manager and future colleagues of the candidate, to be mentally prepared for the change that comes with getting new people on the team.

The pace of talent acquisition relies on factors such as market conditions, the company's industry, and the uniqueness of the role. In high-speed talent acquisition, it is good to reflect on how the acquisitions turn out, especially around positional fit, cultural fit, talent retention, and long-term impact on enterprise value. Those crucial factors don't tend to align well when the process is rushed.

Acquiring level 1 leaders, of course, should require the longest runway—at least ninety to 120 days. In some cases, finding a CEO can take much longer, but in estimating timelines, avoid using anything shorter than ninety days for your C-suite leaders. Occasionally a level 1 hiring timeline of fewer than ninety days may be possible, but many stars have to quickly align for it to work. Getting lucky is not a strategy. For the CEO's direct reports, I recommend sixty to ninety days. The upper end of the range is a much better approximation, allowing time for the new hires to transition from their current roles. Level 3 hires require forty-five to sixty days. Here, because of the higher supply volume of potential candidates, there is a possibility of higher acquisition velocity. The level 4 positions and beyond, depending on the role and the industry, can sometimes be filled in thirty to forty-five days.

Top-down company-level prioritization, through the lens of magnitude, volume, and velocity of change, gives companies the ability to align their strategic objectives with their human capital needs. This sets you, your organization, and the new hired teammates up for success.

KEY TAKEAWAYS

✓ It is critical to make conscious business choices around the level of overall human capital change a company (and its people) can process and absorb.

✓ Choosing the seniority and number of new hires that can be successfully acquired and crossboarded is key to not overburden the organization and its culture with unmanageable change.

✓ Talent acquisition simply takes time; rushing to make hiring decisions will likely lead to unfavorable outcomes. Allow your company the runway for the right level of diligence to get the right people.

CHAPTER 3

ALIGN RESOURCES

THE FINAL STEP IN YOUR top-down planning is to align resources to support the implementation and execution of the Talent Acquisition Funnel for your company. The three key resources for successful, scalable, and consistent implementation of the TAF are your people, practices, and systems.

People

And it all starts with *people*. A company needs good people to hire good people, specifically people who have the experience, skills, and accountability to lead the entire talent acquisition process. Here are the two questions your company should answer: Who is going to own the TAF and lead the process? This is your champion. Who are all the people who will be involved in the process? This is your hiring team, which could vary in its makeup based on the role being filled.

THE TALENT ACQUISITION CHAMPION

A talent acquisition champion intimately understands the value of people, owns the talent acquisition processes and tools, and enjoys the responsibility of building high-performing teams. In many companies, CEOs are (and should be) responsible for acquiring talent, especially in senior strategic and operational roles. However, as companies scale, those CEOs who figure out how to become comfortable with the lack of absolute control generally replace that control with the privilege of mentoring the next generation of team builders and champions. A talent acquisition champion provides the capacity, focus, speed, and eventually a high quality of outcomes that were previously solely the CEO's responsibility. Especially in organizations where the CEO and other executives wear more than one hat, a talent acquisition champion brings tremendous clarity to the company, making it easy to know *who* is leading the recruiting mandate, *what* process they are going to follow, and *how* they are held accountable for the outcomes. The champion can be within your own team, or if you have investors, you may collectively decide someone on their side could be your champion. This champion is typically not hard to find. You may even want to make this role a part of someone's job description.

The talent acquisition champion should have hired people before (either onto their own teams or on behalf of a company) and should have a strong track record of building and retaining high-performing teams. They must enjoy working with people and should have a high level of emotional intelligence to thoughtfully engage with executives, hiring managers, and candidates. The best champions are also the ones who are well respected and liked within the organization; other employees feel comfortable speaking with them, getting their support, and seeking their counsel. The ideal talent acquisition champion intimately understands the current culture of the company, as well as the culture you, as a leader, are trying to maintain or even build; this intimacy allows them to correctly represent the values of the company and to identify candidates who share those values.

Champions are strong in both process and project management skills, which allow them to drive consistent implementation; maintain a high degree of compliance, process tracking, and measurement of results; evolve with scale; and, as much as possible, remove ad hoc actions or biases of the hiring team involved in the process.

Acquiring talent with the necessary sense of urgency while ensuring a consistent process is key to winning the talent war. A strong talent acquisition champion can be a massive competitive advantage, allowing you to not only win the talent war but also successfully deliver on the strategic short- and medium-term goals of the company related to people and growth.

Caesar Sengupta, CEO of Singapore-based Arta Finance, shared:

One bit of advice that I have received from a number of mentors and friends is that a CEO needs to ask what is it that only they can do and then, if possible, delegate the rest. While I have not quite followed this very diligently, I keep reminding myself of it while making decisions and try to pick up only those things that I know will move the ball for my company. To that point, we invested in a dedicated talent acquisition resource from the very beginning of the company. It has fundamentally helped us scale rapidly to be the global business we are today.[1]

Table 3.1. Examples of talent acquisition champion by company size

Company size	Potential talent acquisition champion
Less than 10 FTEs	Founder, CEO
10–25 FTEs	Founder, CEO, COO/Head of Ops
25–100 FTEs	COO/Head of Ops, HR Manager
100–250 FTEs	COO/Head of Ops, HR Manager, dedicated talent acquisition champion (full-time position)

Some typical examples of talent acquisition champions at various company sizes are listed in table 3.1.

Crucial for your talent acquisition champion's success is for both you and your leadership team to understand and respect the importance of their role. For them to succeed, you must set them up for success. That includes granting them visibility into the company's growth strategy and human capital needs. Access to the business's short- to medium-term strategy and goals allows the talent acquisition champion to build a comprehensive human capital plan and a set of supporting processes to deliver on that plan, allowing the company to deliver on its strategic vision. They will also need to be given the capacity to focus on the acquisition process. It means encouraging them to leverage the full team and to collaborate with the senior decision-making leaders.

Giving the talent acquisition champion the capacity to take charge of the key people indicators and your company's talent acquisition needs, challenges, and solutions reduces your workload as the

CEO. Handing off that baton creates precious executive capacity that you can use to focus on running and growing the company. But to realize these benefits, you and the rest of the executive team will need to help the champion carve out meaningful capacity to deliver on the company's talent acquisition goals.

ENGAGE YOUR TEAM

Successful execution of the TAF will need the engagement of several cross-functional team members. This unlocks various benefits, such as creating overall capacity in the system: When someone on the hiring team is busy, someone else can be called in, thus maintaining velocity at the same quality of diligence. Some companies leverage junior team members who typically have more scheduling availability to engage in the front end of the funnel steps. This allows the hiring team to process a higher volume of candidates sooner and more quickly. The more senior members of the team can then engage meaningfully with select candidates deeper into the funnel, where prior hiring experience and analysis-based high-speed decision-making skills are essential.

Having *more than* two or three stakeholders involved can also lead to incremental insights and perspectives on both the candidates and the talent acquisition process. Collective engagement creates genuine thought partnership within the team, increases transparency across the organization, and allows nonexecutive team members to learn about acquiring and crossboarding new talent. This richer engagement in a high-impact company process increases skill and appreciation, but it is also a great retention tool. Employees feel valued when they are brought into critical company processes alongside senior decision-makers, which not only offers otherwise limited exposure to the senior team but also builds connective tissue across the company and serves as a training tool for future leaders who will need to eventually own and lead the process of building their own high-performing teams.

Natasha DesRuisseaux, Lead of Emerging Creators at Meta's NORAM division, explained how this works within her team:

> I am in the creative entertainment and tech world, where there is a lot of cross-functional work with many of the roles. I have a relatively small team, so I try to engage as many of them as possible when interviewing candidates. It not only helps me save time, but it also gives me insights about my own team's style and how they think about people. Also, it's a great way to coach the junior folks on recruiting and what to look for in new candidates.[2]

Candidates also value interacting with the broader team beyond the executives. It allows them to meet many more employees and empowers them to do their own diligence on the company and its culture. The interaction also provides an opportunity for a much better alignment of values and operating practices, as both parties get to learn about the other as much as possible, increasing the likelihood of a good partnership.

At McKinsey and Company, a global management consulting firm that hires hundreds of talented people each year, the interview process engages everyone from recent hires to senior partners, and each person has an equal voice at the decision table. This level of engagement not only allows junior team members to learn the process, contribute to the firm, and feel valued and empowered but also gives them an opportunity to learn how senior consultants evaluate talent and try to shape the future of the firm.

Your talent acquisition champion needs access to you and other senior decision-making leaders to execute at high velocity. Such access allows them to efficiently iterate on required skills and qualifications, strategic candidate choices, and their ability to get interviews done on time. It increases decision-making speed, and eventually allows the company to close on candidates quickly.

Finally, your talent acquisition champion will need space and autonomy to own the process, engage with the market, and execute on key steps of the TAF. While they are custodians of the company's processes, without a high level of autonomy on items such as market making, engaging with candidates, and hiring third-party vendors, the champion will not be able to move at the required and expected speed.

LEVERAGE YOUR INVESTORS

Certain companies, at some point in their growth journey, realize that they need additional capital to accelerate growth. This is where external investors come into play. As custodians of capital, most investors with a meaningful stake in a business want to engage with management both because of their passion in helping build businesses and to ensure an adequate return on their invested capital. That being said, there is no playbook for CEOs, their teams, and investors to work together. Some parties figure out a great working relationship, while others struggle. It was only when I got to sit in the shoes of an investor that I realized the power of this partnership. Having been an operator in a private-equity-backed business and then sitting on the other side of the table, I realized why there is often a disconnect between the two parties on engagement dynamics and how to bridge that gap. The key insight for me was that investors who go beyond capital to provide operational support to their portfolio companies can accelerate value creation. However, without a genuine partnership, that becomes difficult to achieve.

Most investors have direct knowledge of how to build management teams, especially at the executive and leadership levels. Where they need external support, they can leverage their network to find experts to help build teams. Some investors with prior operating experience can also provide tactical operational support to the CEO when it comes to executive acquisitions, including process design, introductions to recruiting partners, and even potential candidates.

As Josh Finifter, Managing Director at Access Holdings, a US-based private equity fund, explained:

> As a private equity investor, I invest in growth companies, and part of my job is to help our CEOs build high-performing teams. As investors, we know that while capital fuels growth, people build companies. This is why I always encourage operators to leverage us when building and executing on their human capital plans.[3]

It is incumbent on both the company and the investor to have an open dialogue where and when such support and help is most powerful and how each party would like to engage during the talent acquisition process. Without such clarity in both *what* and *how*, this partnership's strength may be underutilized or expectations will be misaligned. There are three key areas where investors and their board representatives can help your business with talent:

organizational strategy and design, the acquisition of talent, and the retention of talent.

Organizational Strategy and Design

Investors who have successfully built multiple management teams will be a terrific thought partner to you as you not only design your organization to meet short-term goals but also plan for long-term value creation ideas. They can support in connecting your growth strategy to human capital plans; designing your short- and long-term organizational structures and compensation plans; gaining market insights on roles, titles, and incentives; and providing guidance on your reporting structures.

Good investors can—and should—help your company hire for the long term. They are not there to manage your operations, but they can help you think through these elements, accelerating the execution of your growth and human capital strategies. They can help you find talent ahead of transformational change initiatives, support and encourage you in adding people sooner than you may have done on your own, or perhaps add roles and capabilities you would have not even considered.

Talent Acquisition

Many private equity funds, family offices, and even VC funds have made a conscious effort to build the operational arms of their firms. For example, many bulge bracket private equity firms such as KKR, TPG, Francisco Partners, Bain Capital, and several others have dedicated operational resources to support their portfolio companies. Many investors in the midmarket and lower midmarket segment of private equity have also built such capabilities to support their investments.

Their aim is twofold: to differentiate themselves from those who don't have such an offering and to genuinely help with value creation inside their investment to amplify and accelerate returns.

Investors or board members are likely to know people who could be a suitable fit for some of the jobs, particularly at the senior management level. Whether it is succession planning, your direct reports, or other members of your broader team, it is always beneficial to let your investment partners know all the roles that you are looking to fill and to give them the opportunity to suggest potential candidates. This does not mean that you don't run the rest of the funnel's diligence steps, but it could save you some time and cost, especially in the market-making step of the Execution stage of your TAF.

I was recently speaking with senior partners of a New York–based private equity fund that was making a minority investment in a services business in LA. The fund's managers had prior experience investing in multiple B2B service businesses and built a strong track record of knowing the right folks within the same industry. During the transaction, the CEO clearly articulated the need to have a strong finance leader in the business. The parties agreed to hire a seasoned CFO, and the fund was able to recommend a third-party recruiting firm to run the CFO search. In addition to identifying the recruiting firm, they were also able to add names of key industry-specific finance executives who could be ideal candidates for the role. The benefits were twofold. First, the recruiting firm had a starter list of candidates even before they formally kicked off the search. Second, they were able to examine the backgrounds of these ideal candidates to develop a benchmark to refer to when they began speaking with others in the market. The result of this network effect was a highly focused and eventually very successful placement of a CFO into the business within sixty days of the transaction closing.

In addition to introducing your company to potential candidates, most investment firms have a reasonably well-developed network of recruiting partners. Recruiting partners can be incredibly useful, especially when it comes to hiring C-level executives. We discuss this in detail as part of the Prepare stage of the TAF.

Depending on their philosophy and capacity, investors will ideally be heavily engaged in your talent acquisition process, especially for level 1 and 2 employees, since they likely have experience in hiring managers into various roles across multiple organizations and also because these are expensive roles that have a significant impact on the P&L of the business. In the case of hiring executives into the company, many investors can augment the management team's capacity by interviewing candidates, and in some situations investors are willing to even lead the entire process in lieu of your talent acquisition champion. As a private equity investor, I often found myself doing just that for many of my portfolio companies, because most of my CEOs and GMs simply could not afford to get distracted from their day job. If you are looking to bring on a senior team member, there is a good chance that the candidates will interface with your board or investors. Involving your investors in the process is beneficial for them, because they can better understand the supply side of the talent market and get to know the final candidate. This also distributes the burden of effort among all individuals involved with the governance of the business.

Getting comfortable with the high cost of acquiring top talent does not come easy to many founders and business owners. Those folks are likely to have done many of the tasks in the organization for a long time and often feel that the price is too high, and ROI too low, to hire someone else. Such thinking holds them back from investing in the business, often leading to dampened business growth. Investors, by definition, are used to putting up capital to help bring in additional talent to help grow a company. As a CEO, you can benefit immensely from such a mindset, as it will help you become more comfortable—or realistic—in awarding the salaries necessary to attract and retain top talent. Also, CEOs and founders often think that they must heavily rely on cash—salary—to make this happen, but there are other ways to help drive up the value of your offer. Investors can get very creative when it comes to incentive design (covered in detail in the Prepare stage of the TAF) and can help you develop such structures to beat the market and acquire great talent.

As your company scales, the need for you to let go of tasks may become challenging. In fact, I have seen many CEOs, who have businesses making millions of dollars in EBITDA with double-digit staff, continue to hang on to tactical day-to-day activities that they used to handle many years ago when they started the company. While I admire the work ethic and the roll-up-your-sleeves attitude, just because you *can* do it does not mean you *should*. The more time you spend signing checks, chasing customer complaints, worrying about the internet, and mailing invoices, the less time you spend thinking about the big picture and realizing that your years of experience and wisdom are best used to help the company prepare for the future. Not to mention that all your interference in daily tasks generally makes the people hired to do that work feel suffocated and even worthless, which can lead some employees to eventually quit.

At some point—either voluntarily through discussions with the investors or involuntarily at the heels of the investors' decision—a day comes when handing over the reins as the CEO is the right thing for the business. While a tough decision, this discussion commands a thoughtful collaborative approach that considers the short- to long-term growth implications, the impact on your employees and customers, and clarity on the skills and experience the next CEO will need. Once again, your board or investors, who would have seen this movie play out, can be instrumental in helping you and the company navigate such transformational leadership change.

When it comes to succession planning and associated hiring needs, investors first start by working with the incumbent leadership to develop the right transition strategies. Fulfilling the needs of the incumbent leaders, introducing new leadership, navigating cultural sensitivities, and ensuring focus on employee and customer retention are some of the areas where investors can be helpful as it relates to people management during planned leadership transitions. They can help determine the appropriate timing of such transitions: when and how to execute the transition plan, and how to best engage all internal and external stakeholders. They can help evaluate the opportunities and associated risks, given the magnitude of such a change and its velocity; the company's ability to absorb such a change; and the risk-reward trade-offs for the business. They can also be a coach and mentor to the transitioning leadership, and in select cases introduce you to others who may have gone through such a journey.

Zack Stiefler, Managing Director at US-based private equity firm Gallant Capital, put his role as an investor in these terms:

Investing is all about people. My job is to underwrite the people running a business as much as it is to underwrite the business itself. It is a big part of my job and those around me to help our portfolio companies find best in class talent, especially at the C-level. Our best returns generally come from companies with strong CEOs, where we can collectively build a great team around them. At the end of the day, our goals are aligned when it comes to driving profitability and ROI. But we need talented people in the business to make that happen.[4]

Talent Retention

Apart from this section, I have purposefully kept the focus of this book on talent acquisition, knowing that employee retention is an incredibly important topic that deserves its own dedicated book. However, when it comes to working with your investors, it is important to note that employee and customer retention is a major part of their underwriting and a topic that most investors will have a lot of experience with. The multifaceted—financial, cultural, short-term, and long-term—impact of retention loss can be incredibly dilutive to a company's enterprise value, and it is in everyone's interest to prevent such dilution. For that reason, investors will be motivated to partner with you on defining retention for your business, measuring and tracking it operationally and financially, and defining the processes and policies to foster a retention mindset.

Implementing best practices for talent retention starts with the mindset and culture. Your investors can help develop such a culture through scalable processes and practices that work for your organization. This does not always mean that the investor will have all the answers, but they will either serve as a thought partner or will introduce you to other organizational experts who can help.

Another area where investors can have a huge impact is coaching and mentoring your top team. Contrary to common thinking, top talent requires as much coaching as—and sometimes more than—others. However, coaching top talent may not be as straightforward as coaching others in the company. Those coaching need to strike a careful balance among being their thought partners, giving them autonomy, having the right financial and professional incentives, and also providing mindful oversight to hold them accountable and to help them succeed. There is nothing worse than working with hard-to-find amazing people and then losing them to the market because they felt either micromanaged or abandoned on an island. This can be another very helpful area to get your investors involved, by coaching the top team members directly, introducing them to external coaches and mentors, or sharing tools and third-party programs to support their development.

You're on the Same Side

Most investors use the financial health of the business for the economic underwriting of their investments, but what the majority will tell you is that they are truly underwriting the management team's ability to scale and build the bigger business, leveraging the investor's capital. The higher the investor's confidence in the organization, the management leading it, and their ability to work with management, the more likely an investor will have the opportunity for higher rates of returns. The most enjoyable and one of the most challenging parts for me of being an investor is working with the founders or CEOs to effect change at the C-level. It doesn't matter which hat I have on—CEO, operator, or investor—my confidence in a company's growth and ROI potential is highest when the right group of people are running the business.

The good news is that many investors are also operators; they also need to tackle the talent acquisition problem for themselves and their other portfolio companies. This combined experience can help them help you with organizational design and strategy to guide you through your talent acquisition journey.

Although at times your immediate needs and those of your investors may differ, positive outcomes for the company and the resulting ROI benefits both of you. With your end goals necessarily aligned, it creates a tremendous synergy to maximize the potential of your partnership.

Practices

To help your people implement the TAF, you also need a consistent set of practices. The practice of structure, consistency, discipline, and accountability ensures outcomes are repeatable, reliable, and predictable. This is also true for successful adoption of the TAF. This yields the best ROI from the process, which is what most CEOs, operators, and investors want to achieve.

A *structure* can be as simple as a work plan for each talent acquisition project, which includes workflows, sequencing, timing, communication guidelines, and clarity around ownership. For the work plan, the idea is to take the hire-by date for the role (essentially when the company wishes to have the candidate's first day at work) and work backward to identify the timing for each of the TAF steps. This structure will give the company (and the people involved in the process) clarity on when to expect each step to take place and how to orchestrate the entire process. The communication plan includes any company-specific content being shared with the candidates, such as your current overall financial and operational performance; strategic vision, values, and practices; human capital plan; and specific FAQs about the role. It also includes clarity and alignment around *when* certain information is released and, finally, *who* distributes that information to candidates and third parties, as well as internally.

Be *consistent*. The yield from the TAF significantly improves when there is consistency in the execution of each of its steps—across all candidates applying for a role, as well as across all the roles being filled. Such consistency generates a great amount of high-quality data on both the candidates and the process. Good candidate data improves your diligence and insights while also minimizing the risk of any inherent biases. Good process data allows you to learn from your implementation and find areas of improvement, as well as knowledge of what is working. Companies that do this well ensure that they don't reinvent the process, agnostic of the interviewer or the role being filled. Your talent acquisition champion should play a key role in ensuring compliance across the ranks and consistency in use of all the steps of the funnel.

Consistency brings us to *discipline*. Specifically, it is crucial to stay disciplined in being consistent with the process and across all acquisitions. This develops positive habits. Too often, companies remain consistent for initial acquisitions but quickly lose that discipline. Some of the ways in which these inconsistencies can be spotted include variance in the steps followed; not including standard diligence questions to ensure comparability across candidates; constant changes in who is involved in the diligence process for one role, resulting in incomparable data across interviewers; either a change in or a lack of evaluation and decision-making criteria to measure and rank candidates; and variance in the completion and rigor of reference and background checks. This discipline comes from two places: top-down leadership and empowerment combined with accountability.

This brings us to *accountability*. All of this advice applies to you, as the CEO, as much as it does to your team. Being a CEO or executive leader does not give you a pass from following the processes. When CEOs and other operators consistently demonstrate process discipline, it leads to a much higher level of compliance and adoption by their teams. When you don't, the lack of discipline leads to chaos and frustration among both the team and the candidates and eventually becomes your problem. Be honest with yourself about how disciplined you are in following your TAF, and examine how you can lead the way in implementing a disciplined mindset within your organization. Empowering the talent acquisition champion and other team members to have the decision rights and authority to implement the process will improve team accountability by calling out (respectfully and professionally) those who don't follow the process. No one gets a pass, including you. The excellence of your company's process will not matter if you do not have the discipline to implement it.

Systems

This brings us to the third and final resource needed to implement the TAF: your systems. This is really about consistently using tools that enable you to increase your company's effectiveness and efficiency to close on the top talent quicker than the competition. Tools can help throughout the talent acquisition journey, including with thoroughness of your due diligence, consistency, speed, and scalability.

While many businesses are starting to get creative and savvy with the use of tools, the majority of companies still don't effectively leverage this avenue to augment their capability and capacity. Whether it is an off-the-shelf, third-party system or something your team has developed in-house, the idea is to not get caught up in what the best tool is but to focus on the best tool *for you*—the tool that can get you the best outcome and hence a great return on your investment.

Later in this book, when we get into the Execute stage, the use of leadership and behavioral tools is explored in more detail. These reduce your reliance purely on any one person's instincts or emotional biases, instead providing a more measurable, fact-based dataset for decision-making.

Other TAF steps where you can consider implementing systems or tools include resume review, interview scorecards, candidate calibration, and reference capture. Resume review tools can either help reviewers systematically capture their thoughts on each candidate or can help automate some of that process with AI. Interview scorecards record quick and structured codification of interview scores, allowing faster alignment within the hiring team on key attributes. This further promotes consistent decision-making across interviewers. LinkedIn and Indeed are some of the companies that offer easy-to-use scorecard templates. Candidate calibration tools help you score each candidate on specific traits to give you a record of each interview and allow comparability across candidates. These systems help consider the voice of members of the interview team regardless of their seniority. For those team members conducting the reference checks, a reference capture tool facilitates calibration and reporting of feedback.

Regarding process tools, if you are a small private business that hires fewer than ten people each year, then a homegrown Excel tracker is sufficient to help you navigate the talent pool. On the other hand, if you plan to hire in the double digits each year, then third-party applicant tracking systems might be the way to go.

A company's capabilities get exponentially stronger when it has great people, simple and consistent practices, and reliable and scalable systems. With great people in your business, both employees and investors, and your ability to leverage their skills, you will be able to successfully compete to acquire top talent.

Having consistent practices and systems allows companies to scale reliably while also being able to learn from their mistakes. This becomes a superpower for talent acquisition, as it allows you to remove bottlenecks to rapidly attack a highly competitive talent market while also creating repeatable and measurable outcomes.

KEY TAKEAWAYS

- ✓ A talent acquisition champion creates focus, harnesses collective capacity, and improves the quality of diligence.

- ✓ Beyond providing financial capital, most investors can engage operationally with you and your company to help with talent acquisition. This engagement increases their chance of realizing underwritten returns from the portfolio and can transform your company's capability and capacity.

- ✓ Practicing the use of a simple, structured, disciplined process will increase your yield from the Talent Acquisition Funnel.

- ✓ Systems create capacity and increase distinctiveness. Using tools to gain unbiased additional data on candidates can increase your company's diligence capabilities, and the data from those tools can help triage the candidate pool, creating capacity to focus on fewer candidates.

PREPARE

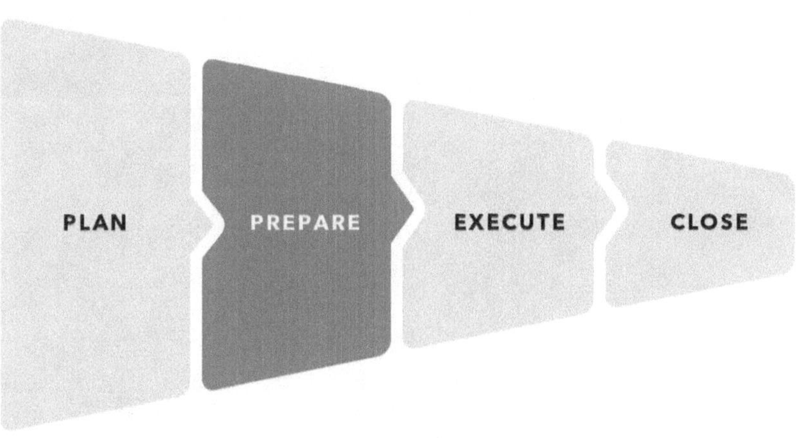

DEFINE THE ROLE

I insist that every one of my team know their why. . . .
Why is their role so critical, and why do they do what they do?
And I do my best to help them understand how that
relates back to the bigger picture for business.

—NICK SAUNDERS, General Manager of Operations
at Landscape Solutions, Australia[1]

MOST EMPLOYEES CONTRIBUTE A significant portion of their lives to their job, with many dedicating at least 50 percent of their day to the company they work for. Many draw positive energy from being part of an organization that has a clear purpose, vision, and mission and having a role in that organization that contributes directly to that purpose. While money is a great motivator, being part of something bigger than themselves, having a purpose at work, and seeing their actions tie directly to the mission of the company can lead to incredible levels of job and life satisfaction. In fact, nearly 70 percent of the CEOs who I interviewed for this book said that vision and purpose were two of the most attractive value propositions for talent to join their company. Talented people joined sooner and stayed longer when they could see how their job was contributing to the bigger purpose of the company. This all makes defining the role a crucial step of the Talent Acquisition Funnel.

Purpose comes through when you communicate with prospective applicants how their role will help deliver your vision, and the job description is often your first opportunity to do this. To win applicants, you'll need to define the purpose of the role, which reveals the purpose of the employee fulfilling the role. The job description should also tie the purpose of the role to the overall purpose and strategy of the business. This focus on purpose tends to get the most eyeballs and increases the chances for a better yield throughout the TAF.

A clear purpose in the job description also allows the candidates to calibrate their expectations (do their skills match the role?) and their application material. This self-filtration improves the quality of qualified candidates in the front end of the TAF during the steps of market building and resume reviews, which means fewer but better candidates in the later stages.

Finally, a clear and pointed job description serves as a frame of reference for the company throughout the talent acquisition process. As the number of candidates increases and the overall hiring process time increases, companies can easily forget what they are solving for with this new hire. During interviews and even the closing stage, it is natural to lose sight of specific requirements from the candidates. Having a North Star document helps declutter the acquisition team's judgment and serves as a settlement guide, especially when there is misalignment on which candidate is better and why. Even after the employee has joined the company, a purposeful job description can be used for performance management. It becomes an ongoing reference document for both the employees and the company to evaluate performance against expectations.

Many companies get tripped up in the tactical aspect of a job description. There are companies that don't even have job descriptions for many roles in their organization. Then in situations where there is a document, it is not clear and purposeful. In some cases, it is a laundry list of catch-all topics from strategic to operational, from day-to-day to long term, and with limited to no connectivity with the company's overall growth strategy and vision. In either scenario, the company misses out on the benefits of a clear alignment of purpose and resulting ROI from the role.

In the TAF, having the job description is a gating item: The role must be clearly defined before the company can even begin to think about how it will go to market to find the right talent. The description connects the role to the human capital plan and therefore to the overall growth strategy of the company, to make it clear *how* the company is going to achieve *what* it is solving for. In this step, your company can handpick the specific initiatives and deliverables from its strategic planning process and place them right into the job description, instantly establishing that connection. The more your company includes elements of its strategic work plan in your job descriptions, the higher the possibility that your new hires will contribute directly to the overall goals of the company. It is almost as if the sum total of all job descriptions and their respective deliverables should equal the list of qualitative and quantitative outcomes established as part of a company's growth strategy.

Finally, the job description should also be viewed as a marketing tool to attract the best possible talent you can find. By leveraging it as a marketing tool, you can amplify your company's market-building efforts and give yourself a real opportunity to create a powerful talent pull. It is always helpful to get someone from your marketing or business development team to add some energizing content into the document to increase the attractiveness of the company and the role. Let us get into the tactical aspects of defining the role and developing a job description where you will notice that every attribute listed in a job description is essential both to the candidate and to the company.

About the Company

While not technically a description of the position, a job listing will include a description of the company. The intention here is to benefit from some honest marketing while also sharing details with the candidates who may not have heard about the organization. This description can be short but should be distinctive—the equivalent of a thirty-second elevator pitch. Some helpful categories that can be described here include your company's purpose (the reason for its existence), ambitions (qualitative and quantitative aspirations), and values or ethos (guiding beliefs, operating principles, distinctive traits).

Most candidates are looking to join companies where there is a high level of value alignment. A job posting is incredibly useful for potential candidates to be able to learn about the company and genuinely imagine themselves being part of the team and adding value to its purpose and vision. While the majority of the candidates will do their own primary research on the company (through websites, social media, Glassdoor, etc.), the company description in the job posting is their first taste of how the company sees itself, the product and service areas it focuses on, and the key aspects of the business it is proud of.

The Purpose of the Role

As discussed earlier, top talent is looking for a purposeful job, and you must clearly build this bridge for them. This is crucial: You should crisply and accurately state the purpose of the role and the purpose the future employee will serve in the job. The question you should answer here is this: What purpose is this role fulfilling as it relates to the company's quantitative and qualitative strategic goals and overall purpose?

Title

From a TAF and market-making perspective, given that most (if not all) candidates search for new jobs based on titles, titling a position can make a big difference in the volume and quality of the candidates who show up at the front end of the funnel. Depending on the market-making avenues and job placement sites your company uses, the job title can be used to channel and target specific candidate segments. Inflated or deflated titles will lead to misleading marketing and poor process outcomes.

For many candidates, a bigger title often leads to validation of success and can be a huge source of pride. While there is a natural correlation between a loftier title and higher compensation needs, I have been part of many conversations where employees and candidates have traded off some increase in compensation for a higher title, given how much it meant to them.

Derived directly from the human capital plan, the title of the role needs to accurately reflect its level (i.e., level 2, level 3) and location (function, division, corporate, executive management, etc.) in the organizational design. The accurate placement of this role is important for your management team to know where and how the role will affect the company, and the location and titling of the role can have a massive impact on the existing employees and the culture of the organization. Not only can misaligned titles for incoming employees create confusion among incumbent employees, but they can also generate resentment and fear, which gets particularly inflamed in situations when you may be offering a title with no precedence in the company. And whenever the title does not correlate well with the job's purpose, deliverables, and requirements, it creates confusion within the candidate pool and can sometimes even generate distrust. None of those feelings encourages candidates to apply, leading to poorer process yield. However, if the title is appropriately paired with the position's purpose and influence, you are likely to increase the pool of qualified candidates because their expectations for the role will be accurate. Additionally, a title appropriately calibrated with the market improves the pool of qualified applicants with similar current titles and those who are wanting to take a step up in their career.

Reporting Lines

In many job descriptions, companies don't bother to indicate who the role reports to. If the work discussed in the previous section is done, then this is very easy to do. The value of determining the reporting structure is that it allows the company to design and implement the organizational structure that supports its growth strategy. It also allows the company's management to align on who will be responsible for the new hire, their development and mentoring needs, and their deliverables.

Clear reporting lines present an opportunity for the company to avoid making the unintentional mistake of having multiple direct bosses over the employee. The idea is to make sure each employee knows who is responsible for their management, development, work assignment, reviews, and mentorship. Having multiple bosses almost always leads to utter confusion for any employee. In most (if not all) such cases, the outcome is eventually pretty much a disaster; in addition to confusion it makes the employee less productive and increasingly unhappy, which can eventually lead to retention loss.

While it may sound like a trivial and sometimes unimportant attribute from an employer's perspective, for employees, knowing who they report to and where their boss is in the overall organizational stack is incredibly powerful. Talented folks want to know how their work is going to affect the business. While clarity on the purpose and deliverables of a position are important, people know that the level of influence they will have in a company is as much a function of what they are doing as it is of where they sit in the organizational stack and who their boss is.

For many roles, reporting lines equate to visibility in the organization. This, in turn, results in their work not only getting noticed but also having a higher possibility of contributing to the overall purpose and vision of the company. You should indicate clearly in the job description to whom the role directly reports and whether there will be any indirect reporting to anyone else in the organization.

Key Deliverables

The job description should also include a list of three or four of the most important and tactical deliverables that this role needs to produce. The more specific the better, as it will help the company tie back to the specific business initiatives that led to its need for this position in the first place. For the candidates, clarity on what they need to produce, both on a recurring basis and with one-time projects, will indicate how they can leverage their background and experiences to get the job done.

For example, for one of my portfolio companies, M&A and the associated restructuring of the business was a major part of the growth strategy. Therefore, when we needed to find a COO, some of their key deliverables included leading integration of acquired companies, organizational redesign, and synergy extraction. In a separate section of the job description, we highlighted what success would look like for the role, which included specific measurable outcomes from the M&A part of their job.

Adam Cooper, CEO of private-equity-backed Oasis Dates, North America's largest date grower, echoed this approach:

> In addition to carefully and thoughtfully defining the purpose of each role so that it is linked to achieving organizational strategy, also define what success looks like for the role. A great way to do this is to outline the four to five year-one individual goals for the role. Then, you can imagine what it would take to meet or exceed expectations on these goals. This outlines the specific things that you have delivered to really move the business forward.[2]

Key Requirements

Here the company must list three to five key requirements in the role, without which it will be incredibly difficult for someone to be successful in the role. These typically include technical or functional skill requirements, leadership requirements, and any number of other items that you determine are specifically required in the role.

Technical requirements are particularly relevant for functional roles such as those in technology, finance and accounting, sales and marketing, and specific operational (production, assembly, Lean Six Sigma) jobs. The specific needs within each should tie back to the strategic needs of the business. Additionally, companies expect successful tenure in technical and functional roles. However, many companies just list the top of the tenure range, which scares candidates away and is often unnecessary. Instead of asking for maximum possible years in a role, if you set the floor with minimum time (using "at least" language) a candidate should have spent doing the type of work (or something similar), the answer changes and it opens your candidate pool at the front of the funnel. The idea here is not to minimize the importance or value of additional years of experience but to consider applicants who may have enough experience to get the job done, are looking to learn more, and are excited to codevelop with the company's growth. Of course, there are times when you need someone to know the topic cold, and although tenure can be a leading indicator of experience and knowledge, the caution is that more time does not always correlate to better knowledge and higher productivity.

For leadership requirements, providing as much specificity as you can share is the best practice. Examples could include the size of the P&L or budget to be managed, the number of people who will be supervised, M&A specific needs, the expected people and customer retention stats under the new hire's leadership, the minimum revenue or EBITDA growth rates to be achieved, any strategic initiatives such as cost management, systems implementation, business restructuring, and other high-priority KPIs to be delivered in the role.

Other crucial requirements to clarify include the geographic location of the role, travel needs, office hours, compliance with the company's remote operating practices, and other key role-specific needs.

Requirements are often seen as cookie-cutter content and therefore undervalued by many employers. However, what most companies don't realize is that by including the above items, this document can be your leading instrument to attract a higher quality and quantity of candidates; therefore it becomes a clear competitive advantage over others who continue to neglect sharing this level of information.

THE EQ MATRIX

As discussed during the prioritization step of the Talent Acquisition Funnel, in addition to the key technical requirements of the role, you will want to think about the level of EQ (emotional intelligence) needed in the person you are hiring so they can successfully effect the changes you wish to introduce in the business. Having clarity on required EQ levels in a role and across the company can significantly affect the velocity and volume of your hiring. Some companies prefer more tenure and industry experience over EQ, while others value people skills more than technical capabilities to make a hiring decision. Such decisions will affect the volume of candidates you are likely to see in the front end of your TAF.

To simplify your decision-making choices, I developed the EQ Matrix (see figure 4.1) that considers the levels of change that the role needs to manage and the level of people skills necessary to effect that change. EQ scores are kept as high-medium-low for simplicity and to avoid false precision with numerical scores.

The intention here is for you to use this matrix to decide the levels of EQ needed in the role and be sure that your hiring team is particularly mindful when the EQ need in the role is high. By having

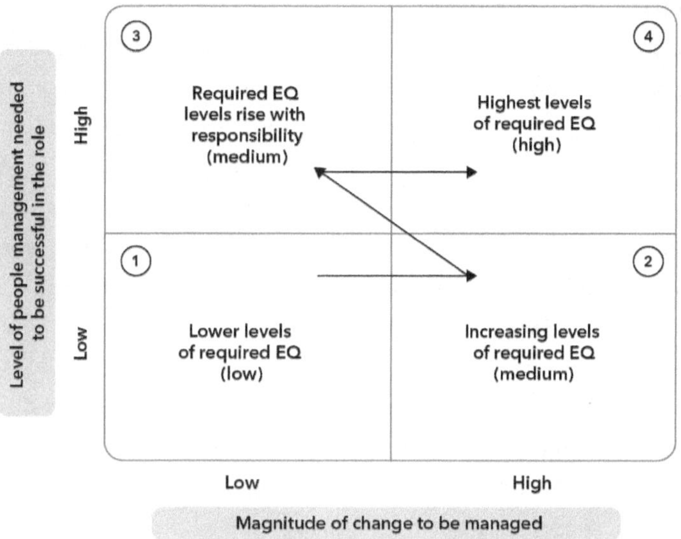

Figure 4.1   Emotional Intelligence Matrix to determine required EQ levels in the job

done this analysis, as the candidates come through the funnel, you and your hiring team will have clarity on the specific people skills you will need to assess.

The lowest score is not zero, as I strongly believe that every person needs *some* level of emotional intelligence to be successful in their job and add value to the organization. Also, increasing the need for people skills does not always correlate to higher titles. EQ is not an isolated requirement for senior members of a team, and while C-level employees need more EQ, an analyst working on an annual budget will need emotional intelligence to partner with, problem-solve with, and even influence functional and divisional leaders on the final product. And most importantly, you must evaluate the cumulative magnitude of change from a company's portfolio of initiatives, including both large and small projects. Large change initiatives, such as M&A, are easier to spot, but companies often underestimate the level of cumulative change from several smaller

continued →

incremental change projects that are either underway or need to be led by the new employee.

Quadrant 1: Low magnitude of change, low requirement of people skills. A company does not have major change management projects, projects already have the appropriate dedicated resources, or the role is not meant to effect big changes. Accordingly, the new employee will likely not be a big change agent, and hence the required level of EQ in the role is low. Also, if the role will not require a person to influence people or manage necessary changes, then the EQ needed will also be low. Both attributes together would suggest that a lower (not zero) EQ employee will be sufficient. Hence, you may plan your hiring to prioritize technically competent candidates rather than focusing on their emotional intelligence.

Quadrant 2: High magnitude of change, low requirement of people skills. A company having a high volume of projects or projects with high magnitude of change will need to acquire people who can help implement and manage that change. However, those roles might be highly executional in nature, limiting the need for significant people skills. Examples include data analysts, web developers, and design engineers.

Quadrant 3: Low magnitude of change, high requirement of people skills. The company may have a few transformational projects that bring change, but the person being hired is required to frequently interact with people (customers, employees, and vendors) or oversee many small-change projects. This will require them to have high EQ. Office and account managers are great examples of such roles.

Quadrant 4: High magnitude of change and required people skills. A role will be placed in this quadrant if the person will not only have a lot of responsibility to manage or oversee the portfolio of major change projects but also need high levels of people skills to influence and implement changes. An interesting irony of placing a role in this quadrant is that hiring a person such as a new CEO (level 1) or their direct reports (level 2s) introduces a big change to the organizational system, and on top of that, their mandate requires them to implement new change programs in the company. This requires the new leader to have significant EQ to manage both drivers of change simultaneously.

Figure 4.2 indicates common roles, based on simplifying generalizations about role definitions, within each quadrant of the EQ Matrix.

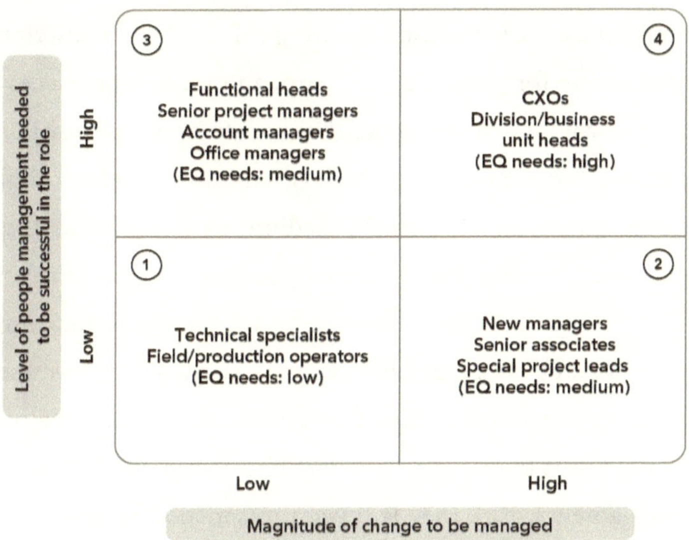

Figure 4.2 EQ Matrix: examples of common roles based on quadrants

Success Criteria

The job description should state what success looks like for the role and specifically what outcomes, if achieved, are going to define success for the employee. This section of the job description, when done properly, will also be tremendously helpful to both the employer and the employee during the annual performance review. Some of the success criteria or metrics will tie back to the key deliverables from the role. The process of identifying and prioritizing how you will measure a new role's success and how that ties to your strategic plans is equally as important to you as it is to your future employee. Up-front clarity of expectations leads to clarity of measurement throughout the employee's tenure with the company. There are a few elements that you should consider when incorporating this in the job description.

The timeline for producing the work and measuring success can be broken down into two buckets. The short term is typically the first ninety or one hundred days in which certain tasks can be completed by the new employee, whereas the medium term represents the first twelve months. In some cases, especially in senior executive roles, it is good to state three-year goals. This can be helpful when your company is working on long-range transformative initiatives that have specific milestones to reach in that time frame. For example, when a private equity fund wants to sell one of its portfolio companies in three years and needs a new CEO, they will want to set specific timelines and milestones (e.g., EBITDA and growth rates) in the job description to ensure clear alignment of expectations with all applicants. Similarly, when searching for an executive to oversee expansion into a new market or a product launch, you will want to highlight measurables/KPIs such as revenue and market share or number of customers, along with timelines, to ensure alignment. Having such aspirations clearly delineated in the job description can provide long-term vision and clarity for top talent joining your team. For the candidates, these goals can be inviting, energizing, and an exciting challenge to take on.

Ideally the job description should include three to five success KPIs that can be tracked and measured. They do not all have to be quantitative, but the outputs must be tangible. Some qualitative examples include opening a new office, building a tech team, hiring a Controller, launching a new performance review program, and implementing a safety process. Quantitative examples might include meeting target levels for profit, revenue, cost, or any other financial metric; getting a set number of acquisitions done in a set time frame while delivering measurable financial synergies; expanding the number of supply side vendors; improving the safety stats of the company; increasing customer satisfaction levels by a target percentage; or improving customer and employee retention stats.

Compensation

In addition to the description and purpose of the role, the job description document should clearly state the compensation the employee can expect to get from the company. Candidates, across the organizational stack, will only apply for roles if they know what the likely remuneration package may look like. It has a few parts, including the base salary, bonuses, and any other incentives relevant to the role.

For base salaries, it is perfectly fine to give a range, footnoting that the quality and experience of the candidate will determine the exact number. For companies who worry about losing downstream negotiating leverage by revealing the number too soon, what you have to believe is that for someone to apply for a position in your company and consider leaving their current salaried position without knowing what the prize is on the other side, one of two things has to be true: Either they need to be in love with your organization's brand, mission, or values, or they need to be desperate for a position. While the former is extremely flattering, most companies I work with don't have the brand cachet to be able to use that as a point of leverage to consistently attract top talent. Similarly, I have not yet met an employer who wants an applicant pool filled with desperate candidates. Either way, by withholding your compensation levels you are sabotaging your talent acquisition process right from the start. The other benefit of putting out directional compensation ranges is to filter out those who have higher remuneration requirements. This saves you a lot of time, and in a capacity-poor world, it is incredibly beneficial to avoid investing hours of your time only to arrive at a point in negotiations where you cannot build a bridge and have to go back to the starting block.

If you plan to offer an annual bonus for the role, then it is extremely helpful to state the value (in dollars or a percentage of the base salary). It is also important to make clear the contingencies on which the bonus payout is dependent. These could include individual or company performance, milestones, commissions on sales, project completion, and so on. While it is important to state the potential bonus levels, you are not required to share all the specifics in this document. A bonus as a form of incentive can also be strategically designed in a way that creates a competitive advantage for the company, but it is perfectly fine if you do not want to give out the exact calculus as long as you have made it clear how much additional upside could be possible for the winning candidate.

If your company has an employee stock or profit-sharing program or if any other longer-term incentives apply to the role, then you should indicate that as part of your compensation offering. At this stage of the process, just mentioning its availability is sufficient. The intention is for the candidates to know various forms of incentives they can expect to participate in so that they can make an informed decision when comparing multiple offers. It is particularly critical that you (when applicable) share this information because just like strate-gic bonus schemes, long-term incentive packages can be a distinctive value proposition that can help you successfully acquire top talent.

Start Date

Finally, the preferred start date is a key bit of information for the world of potential candidates. It helps the company because it not only ties to the human capital plan but, more importantly, given the tie to strategic outcomes, influences the likelihood of reaching the quantitative and qualitative goals the company wishes to achieve as part of its growth strategy.

What all the elements discussed in this chapter have in common is that their inclusion in any role's definition keeps it accurate, appropriate, and transparent. When described well, while short and direct, these elements will speak to the right candidates and improve the quality of applicants in the front end of your Talent Acquisition Funnel. The job description communicates your expectations for the role but also for the applicant's level of influence in your company and for how they will interact with their new colleagues. That clarity is indispensable.

KEY TAKEAWAYS

✓ Talented people are motivated by the purpose they serve in an organization and need clarity around this to consider joining a new organization.

✓ As opposed to having a laundry list of catch-all to-dos, the job description should reflect the actual deliverables that the candidate will be expected to produce in the role.

✓ Titles and reporting lines are crucial not only for the company but also for the candidate, so they can evaluate their relative position in the company's organizational stack, how that can create leverage and generate impact, and the influence their title will bring both within and outside the company.

✓ Each employee, from the CEO down, should have clarity about what success looks like in their job and how it gets measured.

CHAPTER 5

DESIGN INCENTIVES

INCENTIVES ARE A POWERFUL TOOL to ensure both the business and its people share the benefits of creating enterprise value. However, designing incentives can sometimes be a complicated and even a sensitive affair. Whether it is the executive management trying to design incentives for the rest of the organization or an investor trying to do the same for executive management, designing incentives that are tied to the growth strategy of the business and an individual's role can create tremendous synergies that benefit both parties. By the same token, given how much can be at stake with such incentives, this topic has the potential of becoming heated quite quickly.

Mark Sinatra, CEO of US-based Aspen HR, an eight-time Inc. 5000 CEO, and a seasoned investor, put it this way:

> Incentive design is complex, and one size does not fit all. It is as much about motivating the employees as it is about the company benefiting from their work. The art is to balance sharing the upside with the team but also leaving enough on the table to allow for the next bite of the apple.[1]

While context and details are key to designing incentives, there are some fundamental principles and practices that employers need to keep in mind to ensure incentives work for both the employee and the employer.

Designing incentives for a team always starts with the same question: "What are you solving for?" Without such clarity, it is practically impossible to design something that not only will affect an employee's behavior and their work product but also has the potential to affect an entire organization's culture and its short- and long-term enterprise value.

At this stage of the Talent Acquisition Funnel, you are solving for attracting the top talent that you can genuinely afford, to inspire them to deliver the desired results, and to build or maintain a competitive advantage. To attract top talent to apply for the role and keep them excited throughout the process, you need a clear incentive framework that you can share with candidates as they move through the funnel. While the majority (if not all) of the structure should remain consistent through the process, there is a reasonable possibility that, during the negotiations as part of the Close stage of the funnel, edits and alterations may have to be made to close the deal. I have seen many companies dig their heels in to stick too closely to their favorite structure, lose sight of what they are solving for, and eventually lose the candidate they worked so hard to find. Far too often, stubbornness gets in the way of doing good business.

The good news is that for most full-time roles, some of the fundamental variables of the incentive framework are reasonably simple. The tricky part is that, depending on the role and your company's strategic intentions, these aspects will need to be tailored to serve your needs, including the ability to attract and retain talent.

Base Salary

The first thing a candidate wants to hear about is their salary, so a clear view on base annual salary for the role is key to attracting the right talent. This does not need to be a singular number but can be a range your company is willing to offer, depending on the capability and fit of the winning candidate at the end of the Talent Acquisition Funnel. Now, this may sound obvious, but many management teams often make the following mistakes, which can be easily avoided, right off the bat.

First, they don't have the base salary figured out when they go to market with the opportunity. They are hoping to get to talk to the candidates and see what it would take to get someone to join the team and then work backward to see if they can afford the ask. The reality is that candidates want to know what the company is willing to pay. Trying to do market research by talking to potential candidates is a great way to not only lose credibility in the market but also lose the market itself.

Most candidates have a compensation number in their mind commensurate with their view of the market value of their skills and experience. When CEOs or investors don't do their homework on market rates, and either withhold numbers or offer below-market levels, the result is either no applicants or applicants far junior to the requirements, as well as a longer acquisition timeline and, eventually, a delayed value creation effort for the company.

Instead, you should have a clear, validated figure in mind, and you should share at least a range with your candidates. A fair market value—not to mention the transparency of sharing your number without making the candidate guess—will build trust early in the process.

Bonuses

The next thing that most candidates expect (especially for senior roles) is some form of bonus that is generally expected to be paid out at the end of the fiscal year. This is another market-based expectation, and a job opportunity without this component is going to get less traction and ultimately poor yield. At this stage in the process, you should be able to state whether you will offer a bonus payout in addition to the annual base salary and what that payout range could look like.

There are essentially four simplifying approaches that you and the candidates (eventually employees) can use to determine *what* the maximum target annual bonus number is going to be for them. You can mix and match some of these approaches based on the role, affordability, candidate's needs, and final negotiations with the offeree. Commonly, the bonus is simply stated as a percentage of the annual base salary being offered for the role. In some cases, such as sales, the bonus can refer to the commissions that are often (not always) paid out as a percentage of the sale. Then there is the use of the fixed cash bonus (either in addition to the percentage or instead of it) that gets paid out at the end of the fiscal year. In select cases, you can also offer signing bonuses to attract top talent; such a bonus is paid out when the candidate signs the offer letter or contract (as appropriate).

Another approach you can leverage is role dependent where you can design bonuses based on the seniority of the role, responsibilities of the position, and criticality of their function. Such bonuses can be strategically designed to keep fixed costs down while ensuring executives are competitively compensated. Some companies offer the same bonus percentage across all roles while others may offer higher percentages for senior folks, primarily to increase the variable component of their compensation commensurate with the influence they have on the company's overall performance. The more senior the person, the higher the impact they are likely to have on the company, and these employees wish to benefit from the company's financial upside based on their efforts and responsibilities.

Finally, tenure- or time-based banding of employees is another option for you where, as employees move past certain tenure thresholds, there is a change in the tier or band in which their bonuses are calculated. These are essentially used as retention tools to reward employees to stay longer while also acknowledging their contribution to the company and performance in their roles.

Once you have identified what you want to offer as the bonus structure, the next step involves *how* the target number will be achieved by the future employee. There are two components in line with how most people work: *quantitative* and *qualitative*. The *quantitative* items or variables that can be measured and tracked through the course of the year include the company's or business unit's financial metrics such as target increases in revenue and EBITDA, cost management relative to the budget resulting in specific margin gains, and role- and responsibility-specific KPIs such as increasing customer or employee retention by a target percentage. The *qualitative* variables, despite being hard to measure and track, belong to projects (or milestones within them) that improve the company's overall performance, culture, or long-term enterprise value. They could include completion of company-level projects such as setting up a new branch or office; implementation of the TAF, CRM, or ERP; completion of professional development courses; or launch of a new product or marketing campaign.

It is up to you to choose how to mathematically split the total target between quantitative and qualitative variables. But as a general guideline, I suggest that you start with 70 to 80 percent attribution to the quantitative aspect and 20 to 30 percent to the qualitative pieces, and then apply your judgment on how closely that reflects the company's annual goals as well as the candidate's roles and responsibilities.

The final piece of the incentive puzzle is the set of categories that can be used to inform each of the quantitative and qualitative components above. First is based on a company's performance. This is one of my preferred elements in the overall bonus scheme. When the company (as a collective) reaches its desired financial goals, bonuses get paid out. How much of the bonus is tied to payout levels is entirely up to you. To keep things simple, I use a binary philosophy. If the company equals or beats its overall EBITDA target (it can also be revenue, gross margin, or a combination of the three), then everyone is eligible for a bonus; if they miss the target, then no one is eligible. In the latter scenario, bonuses can be entirely at your discretion as the CEO. Also, alignment with the company's performance maintains alignment across the entire organization, as it creates a sense of equality among the team. You and your executive team can always choose to play with this variable and decide other threshold values when bonuses could be earned or who could be included in such a scheme. For example, you could decide that when the company hits 90 percent of its goal, the team or an executive would qualify for a bonus. Similarly, to allow for unique market or customer disruptions that may lead to missed budgets, you could allow for some exception rules that get triggered.

Figures 5.1 to 5.3 offer directional examples of incentive designs for various roles.

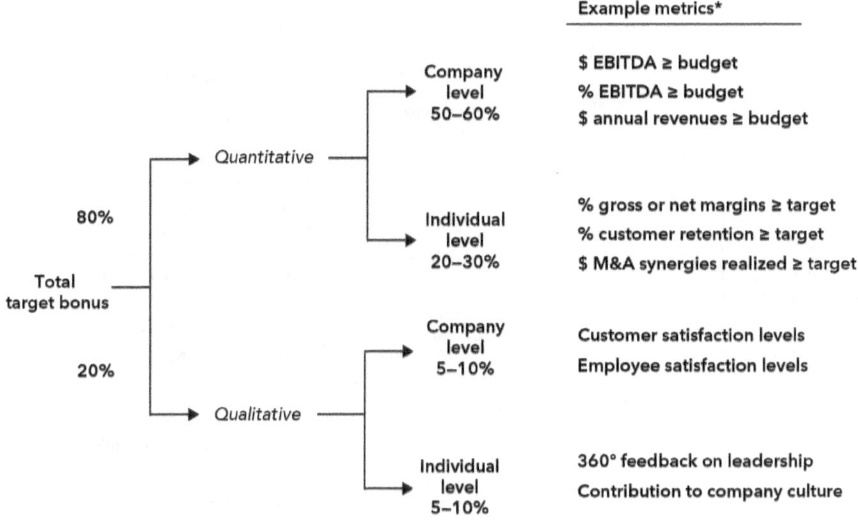

Figure 5.1   Example incentive structure for a COO

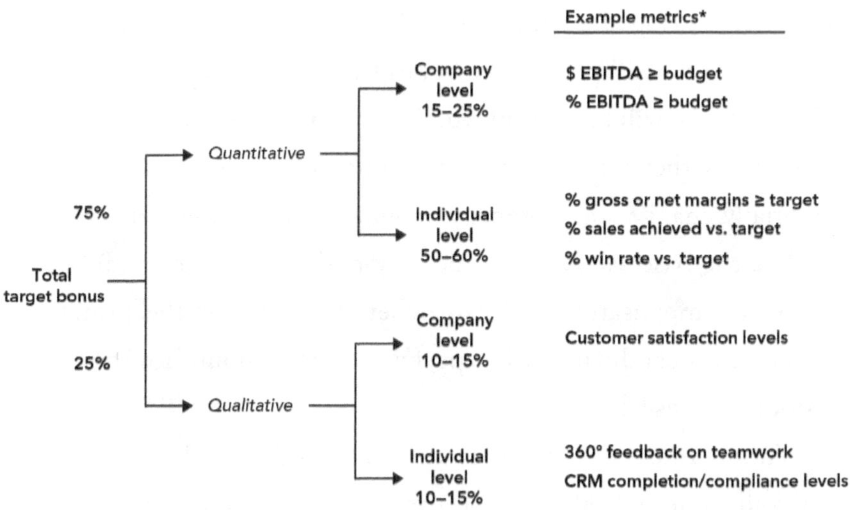

Figure 5.2   Example incentive structure for a salesperson

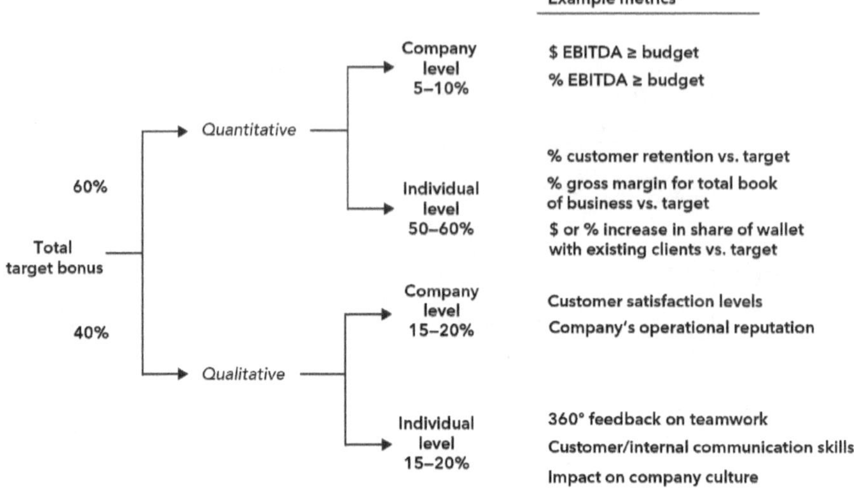

Figure 5.3   Example incentive structure for an account manager

In situations where you are likely to have an employee join the company during the fiscal year, it is important to know whether your company will prorate the bonus based on the amount of time the candidate will have spent working for the company in that fiscal year or whether there is a different policy. Clarity on this can substantially change your company's ability to attract the right talent. Unless the base salary is significantly higher than the candidate's current compensation and can offset the need for the prorated bonus, most candidates will expect a prorated amount for the time worked in a fiscal year.

Another item important for candidates and hence key to closing on your preferred talent is the timing of when bonuses get paid. Many companies are not very transparent with candidates about when the actual cash from a bonus will hit the bank. Once again, clarity up front can be enormously helpful for the candidates to make personal financial adjustments to accommodate any variance in the timing of bonus payout relative to what they are used to. For instance, some companies pay out bonuses by the end of the calendar year. Other companies wait for a third party to audit the financials, in which case bonuses are paid out a month or two after such audits are complete. Whatever your company's policy, it is crucial to make it clear to the candidate.

Some companies choose to only pay bonuses to employees on the condition that they are still employed by the end of the fiscal year. This allows them to use bonuses as a carrot for retention. That said, other companies acknowledge the work of their employees (especially more senior members) and are willing to pay out pro-rated bonuses in the event the employee leaves voluntarily and is in good standing with the company. Whatever the company policy and preference may be, I strongly encourage you to make those abundantly clear to the candidates early enough in the process so they are not stumped when the written docs are presented at the time of hiring or after joining.

Given the increasingly nonlocal nature of talent acquisition, it is possible that your future employee has to move to a new location for the job. To facilitate the move and as a competitive value proposition, many companies offer to reimburse relocation expenses. While technically not a bonus, it is a one-time sweetener companies offer to acquire top talent. What gets covered in the relocation expense is determined by your company's policy, the needs of the candidate, the market conditions, and ultimately what you end up negotiating with the offeree. In most cases, this expense is a fixed amount to be used by the employee for specific predefined categories and is only payable to the employee upon presentation of receipts. In negotiated cases, companies pay out this amount at the same time as the employee's first year bonus. Details aside, if the company is clear about where it wishes to have the employee work and how it chooses to pursue the talent supply market, then having additional clarity on the topics of relocation payment, the payment ceiling for relocation, and the expense categories allowed will help attract more candidates to the front end of the Talent Acquisition Funnel.

Renee Rump, a seasoned private equity operator and the CEO of Heads Up Technologies, USA, summed it up:

> Designing incentives is tricky. My biggest rule of thumb is to keep it simple, as that makes it easy to implement and for the employees to understand. Not to mention it makes our life easier when the time comes to calculate distributions.[2]

Equity

A lot of companies use the word *equity* as a proxy for *long-term incentives* (LTI). The word *equity* may be technically correct in some instances, where the company is in fact offering equity in the business, but the term can often be misused. I prefer *long-term incentive units* because this common term encompasses all forms of incentive plans and instruments that allow an individual to participate in and benefit from long-term value creation in a company. This is an extremely complex topic whose nuances are, alas, beyond the scope of this book. That said, it is one of the most powerful acquisition tools that employers use, particularly for senior management. However, this incentive can also be used for other members of your teams. Here are some key questions that I encourage you to think through.

First, you must decide whether your company is going to offer any form of long-term incentives for the role. Being able to signal to the candidate market that the company offers some form of long-term incentives in addition to cash compensation (base and bonus) can be a huge differentiating factor in talent acquisition. Depending on the position, this signals to candidates that the company values its employees and their contributions, believes in its own long-term value, and treats the person in the role as a partner or fellow owner of the company. This offer can be a powerful and attractive value proposition to the candidate especially if your competitors do not offer such incentive programs or the candidate does not participate in them at their current company.

The next item to clarify is the type of format or style of incentive instrument you are willing to offer. While complex instruments exist, some common versions employers use include stock (equity), stock options, and profits interest. Depending on the role, company policy, and final negotiations at the time of close, it is possible to modify the quantity and combination of these instruments.

That brings us to the topic of precedence. Has anyone else in your company previously received such an incentive and in the form you are willing to offer? Having precedence of use of such instruments can be assuring to the candidates, as it signals broader acceptance of the terms. It also helps the company stick to some of the fundamental terms for all employees and dissuade new entrants from trying to negotiate unique deals for themselves.

The amount or quantity of incentive instrument (shares, grants, profit interest units, etc.) is a simple number that can be shared with the candidates as they move through the Talent Acquisition Funnel. However, most candidates will need help interpreting what the number represents. In other words, if someone will get a few thousand units, your company should enumerate what percentage of the total that represents and how it translates into any form of ownership (direct or indirect) and participation in enterprise value.

Early in the TAF, you are not expected to share a lot of details beyond directional value of these incentives. However, as you get into the latter stages, you will want to offer details around how the employee will earn the incentives being offered: whether there is an associated vesting schedule or individual and company performance thresholds, or trigger events that govern the monetization of such units. In most cases, companies have a three-, four-, or five-year vesting period where the employee earns the pro-rata amount of those units over time. At this incentive stage of the TAF, the company simply needs to let the candidates know the vesting schedule (time and amounts) so that their expectations are aligned.

I am often asked, particularly by C-level candidates, whether they should be able to earn more over their time in the company, since they are naturally trying to maximize their compensation through increased long-term incentive units. Companies are generally open to offering more to certain key employees based on tenure, performance, progression, and increasing responsibilities. At this early stage of the TAF, your company simply needs to be able to say yes or no to potential for earning more incentive units, so that the candidates know what to expect going forward.

The pricing and valuation of incentives can be a complex but critical part of the process. Unless the company itself is in financial services, it is best to employ a third-party financial services firm to help with the process. If you have a financial sponsor or investor—such as a private equity or venture capital firm—then they will be able to help you with this and likely will be involved in the decision-making process around incentive units.

To help candidates understand the inherent potential of these units, I strongly recommend that you develop a simple spreadsheet-based tool where you can map out a couple of different valuation scenarios to be shared with select candidates. This comes in handy toward the latter stages of the Talent Acquisition Funnel, when the company has found its future employee and is in the closing stages of negotiations.

One thing I wish I'd known both as an employee and as an employer is that long-term incentives can trigger an immediate tax event for an employee, depending on the nature of the instrument, timing, and so on. It is therefore critical that the candidates understand these implications to avoid disappointment downstream. Most companies generally understand the tax implications of the long-term incentive units they are planning to offer to their future employees. I strongly recommend that you seek appropriate advice from tax lawyers and encourage the winning candidate to get advice from their preferred third party on this topic.

Overall, the most important philosophy around incentive design is to keep it simple. If the design is simple and serves the needs of the business, then it will be easier for management to implement and for employees to understand. When employees understand the incentive program, they know the levers they need to push to maximize value for the company and for themselves. This alignment in value creation lies at the core of incentive design. Striking the right balance between short- and long-term incentive programs while also calibrating with the role and market conditions will give the company the best chance to attract, motivate, and retain top talent.

KEY TAKEAWAYS

✓ A role's base annual salary should be informed by the value the job creates for the company, the market's view on the job (usually based on titles, industry, company size, and stage of business), and an internal calibration of the compensation with incumbent team members to ensure fairness to the existing employees as well as the newcomer.

✓ The most important factors about bonuses for candidates—and talent acquisition and retention—is to have clarity on *what* the bonus amount is, *how* it would be assessed and calculated, and *when* it is paid out.

✓ Offering long-term incentives can be a distinctive advantage for companies who wish to (and can) offer such an incentive to an employee.

CHAPTER 6

DETERMINE YOUR RECRUITING STRATEGY

TRYING TO HIRE GOOD PEOPLE, many of them, and quickly is not easy for most of us. And when you are looking to hire someone critical to your organization, you should never want to shortchange the process. I learned this lesson the hard way. In an honest attempt to save cash for the business, first as an operator and then as an investor, I was trying to do it all on my own. Instead of flying, I crashed and burned. When CEOs own and control the majority of the recruiting process, they either get pulled away from the day-to-day of running the business or they simply run out of capacity. This challenge becomes even greater as the business starts to scale. Similarly, investors overseeing a portfolio of companies run out of bandwidth when they need to reshape multiple management teams simultaneously and make those changes quickly. In either case there is increased need for capacity and capability infusion for effective and efficient talent acquisition.

At this last step of the Prepare stage and before launching into execution mode, your company should be clear about how you plan to approach recruiting. Specifically, you need to determine whether you will do everything in-house or whether you need a third party to help. The decision of whether to include a recruiting firm needs to come from a place of honest self-evaluation, and the questions are simple: Does your company have the internal capability—the skills and experience—to acquire the talent you need? Do you have the capacity to do the work? If the answer to either question is a no, then my strong recommendation is to get some professional help—*right away.*

A recruiting partner can serve as a temporary extension of your company's talent acquisition capability and capacity by removing some tactical items from your hiring team's plate while also providing strategic counsel where necessary. I did not always use recruiting firms to help me out, and I still don't use them for every single person I want to bring on board, but when my analysis suggests a gap in capability or capacity, I am no longer shy about seeking expert help.

One such expert is Samantha Foster, Managing Director and leader of the Global Industrials Practice at talent advisory firm ZRG Partners, USA. She explained:

> The difference maker with companies who successfully engage recruiters is that they understand it is "recruiting," not "choosing," and if they partner with me, then I can help them "recruit" the candidate they like best. If it is a mutually respectful relationship between client and the recruiter, it works so much better.[1]

What Do Recruiters Do?

Many CEOs ask me, "What is the point of these firms? What do they really *do*?" The short answer is they take a portion of your talent acquisition process onto their shoulders—and off of yours. The long answer is that they provide support in several areas that add capacity and capability where you may be short on both. On behalf of their clients, they lead the search process to locate candidates most likely to be successful in the role. Typically, it is up to your company to run the candidates through your talent acquisition process. But when short on capacity, they help you run through select parts of your Talent Acquisition Funnel.

You'll recognize market building as the next step of the TAF. If you decide to hire a recruiting firm for this step, their first deliverable will be to build a market of potential candidates and bring them to your company's door. One key measure of a recruiter's success is the number of truly viable candidates they can bring to the start of the Execution stage—these are candidates who genuinely meet the profile and experience of someone who can be successful in the role.

As part of market building, having someone out in the market actively cultivating a field of candidates creates a natural marketing drive that increases the awareness of your company's brand and the role being offered. The right recruiter will take the time to understand the company's vision, strategy, needs, culture, and challenges to make a market of talented people who meet the technical qualifications and are most likely to meet the role and cultural fit.

The right recruiting firm will partner with you and your executives on both the strategic components of the search and parts of its execution. This includes role definitions, a go-to-market plan, and assistance during the Execution stage. One of the key aspects of their support is to serve as a critical communication channel between the market of candidates and the company. This partnership can provide both a strategic and a competitive advantage to your company. They can offer market-level insights on the supply chain dynamics, market compensation levels, talent availability, the timing of hire, and feedback from potential candidates on the attractiveness of the role at that company. This data can help you calibrate your offering, which is particularly helpful when the search involves many candidates spread across various stages of the process or when there is a highly competitive situation with a low talent supply pool for a very sought-after level of expertise and experience.

Your recruiting partner should complement your internal processes associated with the TAF by providing detailed and consistent project management of the market-facing parts of the process. This should include weekly updates on previously mentioned market insights as well as quantitative funnel metrics, and the likely timing of seeing candidates cross various steps of your TAF. They should present this information in as much or as little detail as you prefer. While the time to hire is an iterative piece, the best practice is to consistently discuss it at each meeting to ensure everyone is driving toward the same start date in alignment with your human capital and strategic plans. This also gives you a clear sense of when you can expect the person to begin in their role and any growth forecasting that needs to be adjusted from potential changes to the likely start dates. As the process moves forward, the recruiting team is responsible for playing liaison between you and the candidates. This includes setting up introductory emails, working with your team to schedule calls or meetings with candidates, and providing feedback to and from the candidates after each round of interactions with them.

Your recruiting partner should provide pipelines and dashboards that keep a tally of the number of candidates that have been identified, the number that have been contacted, and a breakdown of the number of candidates by contact method such as email blasts, direct emails to select candidates, phone calls, video calls, and in-person meetings. They can also provide an organized view of the CV or resume of each candidate, their expected compensation levels including bonus and benefit expectations, any noncompete or other regulatory hurdles, their location preference, their availability to start at a certain date, their involvement in any other competing recruiting processes, and any other candidate-specific needs that are critical at each stage of the process. That gives us these four crucial recruiter deliverables:

- Search for potential candidates
- Market building with interested candidates
- Partner with and support you and your team throughout the TAF process
- Support you in processing individual candidates through the TAF

Depending on your preference and the recruiting firm's capability, contract negotiations with your final candidates are either led directly by your team or by the recruiting firm on your behalf. This choice typically comes down to your capacity, capability, and comfort level. Not every hiring manager has the capacity or is comfortable having the awkward, sometimes tense compensation discussions with the winning candidate.

While thus far we have been discussing the hiring of individuals, some of you may need to acquire a high volume of mid- to junior-level employees, and a recruiter may also be useful to streamline that process for you. In my experience, contingent recruiting firms tend to offer a good value here because high-volume recruiting can be very capacity draining for your team, and the contingent recruiters only get paid when they have found the people you have hired, which improves your ROI both in team capacity saved and in recruiting firm's fees.

Do You Need a Recruiter?

Around the point of honest self-reflection, when companies ask me how they should figure out whether they need help from a recruiter, I go back to the three Cs framework of capability, capacity, and capital. From a capability standpoint, what you are solving for at this stage is the ability to have a high velocity of great-quality candidates at the front of your TAF. Here what you must ask is whether a third-party firm's quality and speed in generating the relevant candidate pool for the role and industry is comparable to (or better than) what your company can do on its own. Having hired dozens of executives across various scales, businesses, and geographies, I know firsthand the enormous capacity it takes to hire just one senior person. Perhaps the most common question I get about recruiting firms is, "Are they worth the cost?" Recruiters are not cheap, and as I mentioned, not every situation requires you to get their help. That said, to make an informed choice, you need to be able to evaluate the trade-offs between hiring a recruiting firm and the cost of the capacity and capability sink of those on your team who will lead the project.

CAPABILITY

In a world where CEOs need great talent immediately, your ability to move quickly without compromising talent quality will become a competitive advantage. The capability to effectively lead the talent acquisition search rests on two elements: experience with where to look, and having processes and systems that facilitate a rapid build of a high-quality candidate pool at the start of your TAF.

Begin with an honest reflection on your company's true capability (people, practices, and systems) to run the entire acquisition process for the roles you are trying to fill. In most organizations, the capability to hire across the entire stack varies significantly. For example, in some companies, the senior management has had a lot of experience hiring middle management or junior staff but not enough experience around hiring functional leadership roles. For example, a CEO may know how to hire a senior salesperson or finance manager but may have never hired a Chief Revenue Officer (CRO) or a CFO.

Ask yourself whether you truly have the in-house capability to hire for such a role. Has anyone on your team hired for a role this important or this senior? If there is no one on your team, is there anyone on your board who has built management teams and is willing to help? If you or someone on your board has hired someone in this role previously, does your organization currently have the people, process, and systems to support the person who will be leading this effort? If the answer to any of these questions is no, your lack of capability will lead to a failed search process. You will need to either bring someone on your team with such capability or get some temporary third-party help to infuse that capability into your company.

CAPACITY

When I was in junior and middle management roles, one of my biggest disappointments was when my bosses struggled to reasonably estimate the capacity of their teams. Whether it was due to a lack of useful data or of recent tactical experience, the outcome was that the work-to-capacity ratio was always higher than the team could manage. This is particularly relevant to talent acquisition because this part of the job is often nonpermanent. Managers (all the way up to the CEO) are expected to accommodate the hiring process into their "real" job. This creates a false sense of capacity when the company tries to determine whether they can add in-house recruiting to their already extensive list of projects.

Ask yourself whether you or your talent acquisition champion personally has (or can create) the capacity to lead this effort without compromising your day-to-day commitments. Can you or your team realistically dedicate the hours necessary to this effort over the next sixty to ninety days? Will you need to pause or slow down any other projects to accommodate the hiring process? What will that slowdown cost the business both in real terms and in missed opportunities in revenue and EBITDA growth? If you plan to delegate some of your responsibilities to accommodate hiring, does the rest of your staff have the capacity to take them on? If the answer to any of these questions is no, you have two options: You will need to either increase your hiring runway (reduce velocity) to allow yourself and your team to catch up on your to-do list, or you will need to stop doing other projects to create capacity. Either way, there will be an impact on the business. To keep things moving, you could create additional capacity through a recruiting firm.

CAPITAL

I won't lie: Recruiting firms can be very expensive, and it is not always financially feasible to hire one. Even so, the right firm's tactical and strategic support can make the difference in the time, costs, output quality, and enterprise value of the company. Therefore, it is often prudent to investigate capital or economic options and carefully analyze whether the costs of doing it yourself are truly worth it. In my experience, for any hires at or above level 3, most organizations should at least evaluate the use of recruiters.

Most recruiting firms are structured in one of two ways. Some are *contingency firms*, meaning their payment is contingent on a successful hire: If and only if the recruiting partner introduces someone to your company *and* you hire the candidate does the recruiter get paid. The typical rate for such services is 20 to 25 percent of the employee's first-year salary. Others are *retained search firms*, which means you pay them an up-front retainer fee for which the recruiting firm commits to finding suitable candidates for the role on a certain timeline. Many firms also offer a warranty of six to twelve months for executive roles, in the event the employee quits or is fired on fair grounds; the recruiting firm will rerun the entire search process without any additional charge. For a retained engagement, the recruiting firm typically charges anywhere from 30 to 33 percent of the employee's first-year cash (base and bonus) compensation. It is important to keep in mind that you may end up going above budget if you have incorrectly assessed the market price for a role or if you find a candidate who is head and shoulders above their competition and know that their value creation will far outweigh the extra cost you would pay to bring them on board.

For Zack Stiefler, Managing Director at private equity firm Gallant Capital, USA, using recruiters is worth the cost:

> I have always used recruiters for C-level hiring. The truth is that my job is to support my management team partners by providing guidance and making strategic investments in them and their businesses. Bringing on a recruiter is just that—a strategic investment that pays off by identifying more, higher-quality candidates than I or my management teams could do on their own and by managing the process so they can focus on growing their businesses. It is a steep cost but one that is worthwhile and pays for itself over time.[2]

At the end of the day, you must believe you genuinely have the capability and capacity to hire the right person for a senior role and are able to do it in the preferred time frame in order to achieve the planned financial, operational, and cultural results. Otherwise, if your honest self-analysis reveals that you do not have such skills, you are much better off hiring a third party to infuse that capability and capacity.

Recruit the Recruiter

Over the years, I have been both a candidate and a client of several recruiting firms. As a client, I sought help as I tried to fill C-level positions and middle-management roles across the private equity funds' portfolio of companies. As an operator, I have partnered with recruiting firms to find a high volume of field staff and fill interim and even temporary project-based roles.

But I learned early in my career that to find the right recruiting partner that can be an extension of your company representing your company's values and goals in the talent acquisition process, you must take the time and follow a disciplined process akin to finding the right talent for the job you are trying to fill. To keep it simple and structured, you can follow the TAF as in the rest of the book; at the end of day, you are looking for talent, albeit in a third party for hire. However, here's a shortened version specific to finding a recruiter.

First, identify your needs based on the position you are hiring for, including if you are looking for a functional or industry expert. Start by seeking out recruiting firms that specialize either in the function or in your industry. For example, if you want to hire a COO in real estate, you should decide if it is more important for the recruiting firms to specialize in COO hiring or to have a firm that specializes in the real estate industry. Some firms do both, and some have dedicated teams for each, but clarity on what's most important to you will help you find the right partner.

Next, search for search firms. Start by pinging your immediate network to see if anyone has recently used a recruiting partner. Ask them whether they have used a firm to hire a similar position to the one you're looking to fill and whether they would recommend that firm. It is always good to round out your network search with an online search on LinkedIn or Google to see which other local or national firms might be suitable.

From your list of recommendations and search results, build a short list of firms that seem to meet your needs, just as you would with candidates for a job position. Just like the principles of the TAF, your goal here is to do diligence to eliminate misaligned firms quickly so you can dedicate more time interviewing a handful of recruiting firms most likely to be able to do the job. For instance, if a firm's website does not mention the types of industries or functions you are most interested in, then there is a good chance they don't cover them. Also, if their website is clunky or unimpressive, then it could be a leading indicator that they may not be structured well or they may struggle to market your company and the role. Finally, find out what you can about their pricing, and eliminate firms that may be too expensive for you. Your detailed diligence starts here, and you can either use your vendor evaluation process (if you have one) or leverage the TAF steps and questions.

Knowing about some common red flags can be helpful in your diligence of the recruiting partner (or any third-party service provider you are exploring). Most people don't pay attention to this data and miss some vital cues. For example, did anyone even respond to your inquiry in that initial call or email? If they did respond but took several business days, perhaps they are either short on capacity or their sense of urgency is low. In either case, they may not make it to the top of your list. Was their response thoughtful and enthusiastic? A poor-quality response at this initial stage means there's a good chance you won't get the level of attention you may be hoping for when the real project starts. Finally, ask yourself whether they have taken ownership of the next step. This is a subtle sign of their project management skills. Ownership includes suggesting specific days and times that they can get on the phone or asking for a time that is convenient for you to speak to them. If there is no indication of any proactive action on their part, they may simply not be excited, and, in the real project, you may have to project manage them. That is not what you want from your recruiting partner.

As you lead the diligence effort, be as specific as you can about what you are solving for; otherwise, it is difficult for any recruiting partner to help you. This exercise helps both CEOs and their teams get clarity on the role, the reason behind needed talent, time sensitivities relative to growth strategy, cultural and geographic sensitivities, and top priorities for the search effort.

At this stage it is reasonable for you to expect the recruiter, similar to other third-party advisors you may have hired, to share their background as a firm and their project team to demonstrate why they are the best fit for the project. You should expect them to share some relevant recent searches to highlight their expertise. This is particularly true and critical in the case of senior executive searches.

Now you can narrow your short list down to one or two. In this round of diligence, identify the recruiting team members who will be running the project day-to-day. You can ask them for a sanitized (to protect client confidentiality) list (in a spreadsheet or Word document) of candidates placed by the recruiting firm in the last eighteen months in similar roles, industries, and size of business. The contents of the report should include the date of placement, which will indicate the recruiter's recent success levels and therefore their knowledge of the current market supply chain dynamics. It should include the title of placement, which can help you ensure that the recruiter not only has relevant experience but also understands the unique dynamics of trying to acquire the level of talent you wish to acquire. It should tell you the size (FTE, revenue, or EBITDA), location (which speaks to geographic expertise), and industry (to make sure the recruiting firm has the relevant industry experience and a likely network of candidates, which would accelerate the process of building the market) of the hiring employer. It should also include a description of the company, such as *B2B service provider* or *OEM for aerospace and defense* or *F&B copacker*. The intent here is to get a more granular sense of the firm's capabilities within the sector, especially if it is important for the role being advertised. Finally, the recruiter's disclosure should include the salary range and other compensation of their recent placements. Most recruiters will be able to give a decent sense of the salaries, but they don't always know how much equity, options, or other forms of LTI (and respective value) were offered to the final candidate. They should be able to share at least whether or not any LTI was offered. Even that bit of information can be very useful to get a sense of the market conditions and for you to calibrate to what it will likely take to acquire talent.

The benefit of this dataset is that if the recruiting firm can share solid and relevant data, then it is good confirmation that they understand the company, the role being offered, and the purpose of the role. The reverse is true if they end up presenting a "successful" dataset that does not speak to the position being filled. It indicates they either don't have the experience or simply did not pay attention to the brief. Either way it's a helpful fact in the selection. You'll also want to confirm the firm's fee structure—contingent or retainer—and a reasonably detailed outline of their work plan.

Your final step is to ask for references from the recruiting firm you are likely to hire. Again, just like with job candidates, most firms will give you references that will speak highly of them, but checking those references is a critical part of your diligence. It is not uncommon to find something out of the ordinary during reference calls that may change your mind or approach with a specific firm. Ask the references when they last worked with the firm. If the firm has given you references from more than eighteen months ago, it should raise a flag that the firm is unwilling or unable to have you speak to a more recent client. Ask the reference why they hired this firm in particular and how many times they have hired them. You can ask which recruiter personnel they worked with; the service or expertise may vary within a firm. Find out what was distinctive about the firm's service and what they could have done better. Importantly, you should ask whether the firm was proactive in leading the project or whether the reference needed to push them. Did they bring a strong slate of candidates, and did the reference end up hiring someone via this search firm? Was the recruiter engaged in closing on the final candidate? Finally, ask for a rating from 0 to 10 on the overall process, whether the reference would hire the firm again.

Help Them Help You

While it is perfectly fine to have a transactional engagement with a third-party firm, I personally find it a lot more enjoyable and productive when there is a genuine partnership between the two parties. In this case the right recruiting partner can not only reduce the challenge of the hiring process but also make you a better informed, prepared, competitively savvy, and successful acquirer of talent.

I learned this the hard way a couple of years ago when I was managing a portfolio of companies where we were rebuilding several management teams simultaneously. For one of the executive searches, I struggled to find the time to invest in my relationship with the recruiting firm. As a result, I failed to provide the right level of engagement and guidance to that recruiting team. Our interactions became progressively tenuous, and the search eventually failed, causing major delays in enterprise value creation. While we eventually relaunched the search, the failed process left me and my team feeling exhausted, and we had also muddied the target market of candidates, which caused challenges for the new project team. Getting it right the first time—finding the right partner, committing to the relationship, and communicating effectively with them—can help you avoid such headaches.

If you do decide to hire a recruiting firm, like any partner, you'll want to first provide clarity and honesty. Without clarity, there is little chance they—or you—will be successful. The recruiting partner will need your help in understanding your needs at both the company and the role level, your company's culture, or your preferences. Make sure they understand your ideal candidate's profile and your industry, as well as the position's location and the required level and breadth of experience. Be up front about the amount of money you can afford, your true likes and dislikes in a team player, your short- and long-term intentions for the role, and other changes in the organization. Share your process with them—whether you are using the full Talent Acquisition Funnel or specific steps. This will not only prevent duplication of efforts (thereby reducing your efficiency) but also clarify the correct ownership of process steps between you and the recruiting firm. The more transparent you can be with your recruiting partner, the more able they will be to truly partner with you and present you the best candidate profiles to review.

One of the biggest mistakes CEOs and operators often make is they hire the recruiting firm and then tell them what to do. If you have hired a recruiter you like and have been able to thoroughly vet their capabilities, let them do their job. Just like you, they are experts at what they do. However, you may need to actively coach them on your company, cultural, and industry-specific needs. But just as you would your teammates, you should hold the recruiting firm accountable to the terms of the search and, when necessary, give some tough love. This goes back to being completely honest and clear with them.

Finally, be an engaged partner. Just because you outsourced the problem does not mean that it's no longer your problem. Remember, you still own your TAF, and the recruiting firm is there to temporarily augment your capabilities. Help your recruiting partner by problem-solving and providing genuine partnership. Although the recruiting firms are technically providing a service, a true respectful partnership model will get consistently better outcomes.

KEY TAKEAWAYS

✓ Before beginning the Execution stage of the TAF, decide whether you will lead the entire Execute stage or whether you will engage a third-party recruiting firm to augment your team's capability and capacity.

✓ While the capital outlay for recruiters can be high, an honest self-evaluation of your capabilities and capacity will help you determine the relative ROI of doing it in-house versus outsourcing it.

✓ Take the time to do a thorough diligence on potential recruiting partners.

✓ The right recruiting partners can bring a ton of capabilities to the company and its search needs: industry-specific talent acquisition expertise and experience, a talent network, compensation intelligence, and process knowledge.

✓ When engaged in the right way, a recruiting firm provides market insights, tactical executional support, management of the candidate pool, and thought partnership during the latter stages of your TAF.

EXECUTE

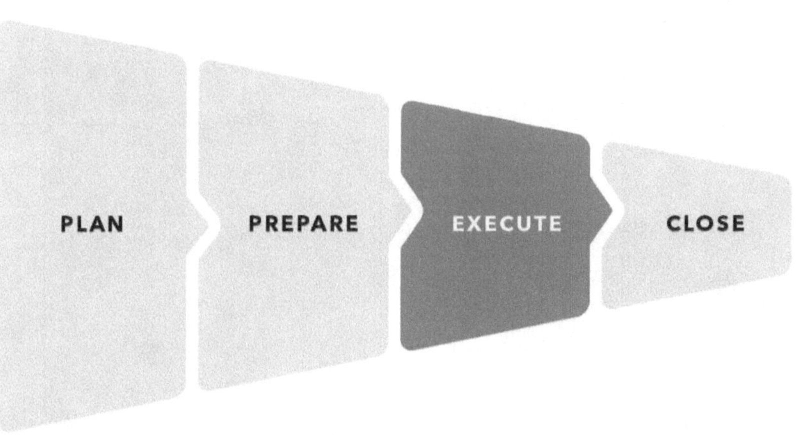

CHAPTER 7

BUILD THE CANDIDATE MARKET

Talent acquisition comes down to execution. As a small business
owner, making sure good quality candidates show up to the process
is the first part of getting execution right. Being clear on who I want
to hire, why, and when allows me to advertise effectively and attract
the right pool of candidates to apply for the job. I cannot afford
to waste time and money, and I have learned that getting this
first step right consistently sets me up for successful hiring.

—DR. ANKIT SHAH, President of Sports and Performance Cardiology,
USA, and Team Cardiologist for USA Swimming[1]

MARKET MAKING KICKS OFF THE execution stage of the Talent
Acquisition Funnel. In some ways, it is one of the most exciting
steps of the funnel. Here, the company gets to market itself and the
job being offered to the world of potential candidates who may or
may not have heard about the company. This is as much a process
as it is a mindset. The intention of this step is akin to a traditional
marketing approach toward customer acquisition, which begins by

increasing awareness of the product or service on offer, with the goal that the target customer segment will buy what the company is selling. In the same sense, your company is aiming to reach candidates, and it is offering (or promoting) a job opportunity (or a purpose) to the market of potential candidates. To be successful at talent acquisition, you and hiring managers must subscribe to the philosophy that they are not the only buyers in this marketplace. You need to sell your opportunity and vision to candidates as much as (if not more than) candidates need to sell their skills and passion for the company's role.

As Shana Plott, CEO of executive search firm Coleman Lew Canny Bowen, USA, explained this stage:

> Building the market for a talent search can be a lot of fun. It's like going on a hunt for this incredible prize, but it takes a tremendous amount of work. We start with a wish list of what the client is looking for and then scour the market of amazing people to find the best of the best who most closely match the ideal profile. Each time, I get to meet new, extraordinary people. It is by far one of the best parts of my job as an executive search consultant.[2]

Market building starts with the job description document, which serves as a powerful marketing tool. In fact, I often encourage companies to engage an internal marketing or business development person to help position the company and role in a way that leverages their market-making expertise and helps the process.

To execute market building, a company can choose one of two options: a light-touch model or a heavy-touch model. In either case, before launching into the market, the company also needs to have clarity on the compensation range and title associated with the role in alignment with the strategic and human capital planning sessions.

With the light-touch model, you are not looking to invest a ton of resources—time and money—into the search. This is a common avenue for most companies. In this case, many companies post the job on a handful of posting platforms such as LinkedIn, Seek, ZipRecruiter, and Indeed. The platform choice often comes down to a combination of the cost (or capital) to advertise on multiple sites, familiarity with the platform (for the talent acquisition champion and the company), and service offerings of the platforms. The biggest benefit of this approach is speed to market, as many of these sites have made posting jobs very simple. After all, this is one of their single biggest value propositions. The second benefit of such locations is that candidates actively looking for new jobs frequent these sites consistently, so these candidates self-select into the jobs and companies they find attractive. For this reason, a post and job description that reflect the distinctive value proposition of your company and the role can be a huge competitive advantage, as they set the first impression for those candidates. The other benefit of the light-touch model is that there is limited strain on your company's resources. Whether the talent acquisition champion or someone else is posting the job, once they go through the initial investment of a few hours to get the posting up on all the chosen sites, their involvement can be quite manageable.

On the other hand, the light-touch model does present a few challenges. First, if the job description is not thorough, clear, and energizing, candidates will click and walk away. The opportunity to interact with the candidates will only arise when someone decides to reach out to show interest. To that point, the light-touch model leads to a reactive approach on the company's part, as you don't know who and when someone will find the posting interesting and reach out. In some cases, a lot of interest can be generated up front that can overwhelm a talent acquisition champion with limited capacity. In other cases, the job posting may take a long time to get noticed and to generate strong levels of interest in the market. Additionally, getting any sort of feedback from the candidate market on the aspects of the job posting they found attractive and the attributes that gave them pause is difficult. Without such market feedback, the talent acquisition champion will not know if a slow response and low interest levels are due to weak talent supply conditions, poor choice of platform, a poorly written job description, bad online reviews of the company, not enough gestation time in the market, poorly chosen keywords that reflect the role, or something else altogether. This lack of feedback prevents the company from making the necessary iterations to increase market interest in the job.

On the other hand, the heavy-touch model entails more active engagement in building a market of candidates. This involves four simple steps (see figure 7.1), beginning with the process of defining the criteria for segmenting the market. This model is similar to the

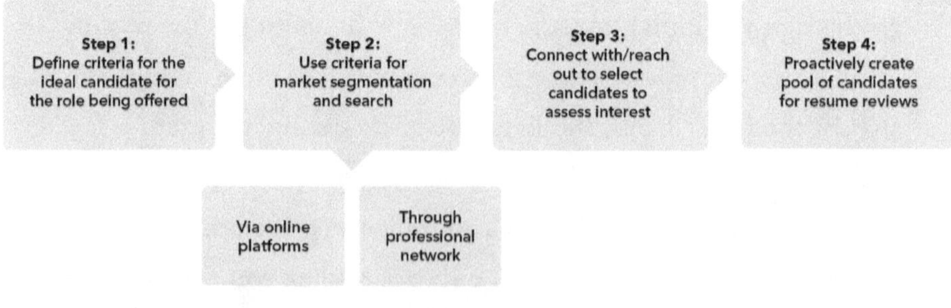

Figure 7.1　Heavy-touch model for building the candidate market

customer segmentation process, in which a company with a specific service or product needs to find the right customer base that is excited to buy the product or service. In the case of talent acquisition, when it comes to market making, the intention is to identify attributes that will help split the target candidate market into subsegments and to market the opportunity to key subsegments (or even at the individual level) that are likely to be attracted to the opportunity and might be best for the role.

Define the Ideal Candidate

You should first identify the critical list of attributes that matter to your search. The next few sections detail three simple ways you can segment the market to identify what you wish to see in the pool of candidates to be interviewed, along with examples of how this translates tactically. It is also possible to layer these parameters on top of each other to really home in on the subsegmentation of ideal candidate profiles. The more refined the criteria, the higher likelihood you will find a candidate close to your ideal. However, the risk associated with a higher level of precision is that the pool of candidates—those who meet all the criteria and are also available and willing to join the company at the price points being offered—gets small very quickly. In other words, the tighter the definition of your ideal candidate, the closer you'll be to a bull's-eye, but be mindful that it will also create a smaller circle of qualified candidates you can pick from. I recommend that you pick two or three priority items and use those to build the market of candidates. This allows a decent level of targeting but prevents the heartache and loss of time and effort that result from chasing a very small ideal candidate pool.

EXPERIENCE-BASED SEGMENTATION

Experience-based segmentation includes the responsibilities and titles the candidate has had and their tenure (present and past).

Their current title should either be the one you are hiring for or one step away from that title. Say, for example, the company is looking for a COO. Ideally, it would be someone who currently has a COO title. However, if a candidate does not have the exact title but is a Head of Operations, EVP, or SVP of Operations, that is also fine. In some select cases, if the candidate is part of a much bigger organization than yours, the CEO, hiring manager, or talent acquisition champion may be comfortable with a VP title. The point of this clarity is to apply specific filters to narrow the search down to specific subsegments of the market. Depending on your company, its culture, and its profile (early stage versus late stage, private versus public), you may choose to engage with more up-and-coming talented candidates—with less tenure—who would grow with the company, or you may decide to only speak to a more seasoned segment of the candidate market.

From a candidate's perspective, if the position being offered is at the same level as or a higher level than their current title, they will likely opt in. If you are targeting candidates who have higher titles than the one you are willing to offer, you will waste both time and money. Only in select cases do candidates entertain the idea of a lower title—typically when they are looking to change industries or they wish to change function and are therefore willing to take a step back in their career to do so; when they are willing to trade down to explore a more interesting business model; or despite a lower title, the compensation they are likely to receive is much higher than in their current position. Outside of these three scenarios, most candidates will likely not even consider a mismatched lower title. If you receive applications from candidates willing to take a step down, I strongly encourage thorough diligence during the interview phase to pressure-test the motivations behind such a move to ensure genuine interest and viability of longer-term employee retention.

While there is often correlation between the levels of responsibility and title and tenure, it is not always guaranteed. Therefore, taking time to specifically dig into this attribute can be very helpful as you try to segment your target candidate market. This process also allows you to clarify key experiences you want to see in the candidate pool. For example, when looking for a C-level executive, this gives you the opportunity to identify your expectations around the size of the P&L they might be handling, the number of business units that they are managing, or the number of FTEs they are responsible for. The magnitude of these numbers (even if directional) can give you a decent sense of the level of responsibility that the candidates currently have. The good news is that many candidates indicate the level of responsibility they wish to take on in their next role. This is often reflected in how they position their current and desired role and responsibilities in the online profiles. This allows you to calibrate your vision for the role both in the short term (what needs to be managed right away) and in the long run (as the company grows).

The type of work they are involved with can be a great indicator of their skill set relative to your needs. This can further refine the pool of candidates to those who appear to be working on projects that resemble what might be required from the role (since this is only based on outside-in diligence). For example, if the job requires the candidate to be able to implement a CRM or to have led M&A

integration work, then a mention of such projects on their online profiles can help you prioritize these candidates over others. Many times, this type of information can be seen on their LinkedIn profiles or is mentioned on their current employer's website (particularly for senior executives). Great candidates are either motivated to add value quickly by applying their experiences and expertise to the requirements of the marketed opportunity or they may get excited by the opportunity to expand their tool kit by taking on a challenge they are unlikely to get elsewhere.

Data on years of industry or company experience is not difficult to find, making tenure-based segmentation relatively easy. However, when poaching talent from high-tenured roles, it is important to keep in mind that it comes with some peculiar trade-offs. Either you can assume that those candidates are incredibly valuable to their employers, making it difficult for you to displace them, or you can hypothesize that they are fatigued and bored, which may make it a lot easier to steal them. From a market-making perspective, it is hard for you to know which of the two scenarios will play out for any candidate. If they have been consistently rising through the ranks, based on their LinkedIn profile or resume, then it may be fair to hypothesize that they are likely to be well appreciated and respected in their organization, making them an even more attractive candidate and hence a definite target for acquisition, but also much harder to steal. As always, great talent is likely to have many options, but that should not deter you from going after them. You must also think through the trade-offs between loyalty and experience across many organizations. Both have tremendous value; you have to decide what matters most to your business.

COMPANY-BASED SEGMENTATION

Specific attributes of the candidate's previous employers can also be used to segment the market. These attributes include the stage (early, late, growth, exit) of those companies, their scale (head count, revenue, profitability, footprint), ownership structure (private, public, private-equity-sponsored, VC-backed), and product or service exposure in line with your company's own current offerings or future needs.

Whether a candidate has worked in small or large organizations can significantly shape their experience, capabilities, and mindset. For many candidates, the opportunity to be part of a bigger company can be an attractive proposition and driver for change. The intention is to avoid a mismatch between your company's scale and the future employee's ability to solve problems at that scale. For instance, if someone has only worked for large-cap public companies where there are tons of resources and incredible infrastructure, then they may not have had the need to roll up their sleeves as much as someone with the same title in a smaller company with less personnel and resources. It does not make them less qualified, but it warrants the question whether they are the right match for the company and if they will be comfortable being scrappy and entrepreneurial in a significantly smaller organization running on a much smaller budget and limited infrastructure. There may also be cultural implications from such a mismatch. For a subset of candidates, the chance to move to a smaller scale can be exciting because either they enjoy building businesses or they get motivated by the challenge of working in smaller organizations where they can get their hands dirty and engage at a much more tactical level than in larger companies. Therefore, how the job description indicates the size of your organization and purpose and impact of the role can shape the size of the talent pool at the front end of the funnel.

Associated with your size, industry, and nature of the role, it may be important for you to know if the candidates have had experience working with early-, growth-, or late-stage companies. In select cases, experience in private or public companies might also help you segment the candidate pool. And finally, for those of you who are running companies backed by financial sponsors, such as private equity or venture capital, it might be useful to find out if the candidates have worked in such investor-backed organizations. The latter is particularly useful for senior roles, where there is likely to be high exposure to investors and where intimate knowledge of the operating characteristics of a sponsor-backed organization can be a differentiating (and necessary) factor between candidates.

Many companies prefer that the candidates come from their industry. However, with increasing competition and reduced talent supply, several companies have strategically started to market jobs to candidates in adjacent industries. In some cases, companies have purposely chosen to bring in talent from a completely different industry to introduce a new way of problem-solving, prioritization, and implementation.

If you are looking to fill a technical role, it is common that many technical candidates like to stick to their industry, where they have built their expertise and enjoy the benefits (compensation, responsibilities, and respect) of their tenure, industry comfort, and earned credibility. When a company from an adjacent or entirely different industry approaches them, the bar for a candidate to move is often much higher. The implication to market making is that you need to be aware and open to the candidates' desire to understand how they can add value and how you believe their skills can be leveraged in a different industry.

LOCATION-BASED SEGMENTATION

As the name suggests, location-based segmentation is important for companies that have specific geographic (local, regional, state, national, or international) needs. However, location is also an important factor to consider based on a company's remote working versus in-office policy.

Based on the strategy work done in the Plan stage of the TAF, clarity around the geographic needs of the role will drive your market-making process. For example, if you want to strategically expand in a new geography and that is one of the primary drivers of the role, then you may choose to market the role only to those who are already present in that region and who will have intimate knowledge of that area's business characteristics. Similarly, if you want to only hire people that are in your state (perhaps because you don't want to deal with multistate employment laws or prefer your team to be co-located), then the market you are trying to build is more tightly defined than if you were location agnostic.

Having clarity around your geographic needs can help you either enjoy the benefits of a well-defined albeit tight candidate pool or take advantage of a larger volume of potential candidates. In both cases you will need to clinically leverage market segmentation and the agility from the TAF to zero in on your preferred candidates. The good news is that most candidates disclose their current location and, in many cases, they are happy to share their flexibility or constraints with relocation. Some candidates have started declaring their travel or work-from-home preferences online or in their applications of interest. This analysis will help you filter out those who may not meet your geographic criteria and thus refine the target market.

Segment the Market

Once you have picked your top two or three preferred criteria for segmenting the market, you can now apply these filters to the various channels at your disposal. These include the online platforms and job boards such as LinkedIn, Seek, Indeed, and Monster, as well as any professional networks you and your management may have. With this step, you get to test the market and figure out how many potential candidates exist that meet the chosen specifications. Often at this stage, companies go through a bit of an iterative process to balance their needs against what the market is willing to offer. This goes back to the earlier point of moving away from the bull's-eye to a point where the company feels it has struck the right balance between its demands and the potential candidate supply from the market.

A Denver, Colorado–based air-conditioning contractor with annual revenue of around $45 million was looking to hire a COO. The company started its segmentation with those specific filters: COOs who have direct experience in the air-conditioning industry and are based in Denver. This led to some hits on LinkedIn, but they realized that the pool of such folks wasn't as big as they had hoped. The company then chose to let go of Denver and expanded to the state of Colorado and eventually to other Rocky Mountain states to find more folks in the pool, as they decided that it was more important to have the industry experience than to have someone local. In this case they could have made an alternative choice based purely on location, in which case they knew they would have had to find their COO candidates from adjacent industries such as the building services segment and be open to folks from plumbing, fire engineering, fire protection, or building construction. While in either strategy, gradually moving away from their bull's-eye would have allowed them to open their target market and find a list of potential people who might be open to a conversation, in this case the management team preferred to get their COO from within their industry. Expanding the geographic reach paid off, as they were able to get a very excited and driven operator from Montana who was happy to relocate their young family for the opportunity to be on the executive team of this growing B2B business.

Connect with Potential Candidates

At this stage, your talent acquisition champion will need to contact the potential market of candidates. This step simply requires the talent acquisition champion to reach out via a cold call, email, or a LinkedIn message. The effectiveness and efficiency of the method chosen largely depends on the preferences of the recipient pool. Some potential candidates prefer to receive calls so they know it is not a scam, but others hate receiving random voicemails. Similarly, a few folks prefer LinkedIn messaging, as it helps them quickly find out more about the sender and the company. Still others are sensitive or cautious of using professional platforms for future opportunities, for fear of somehow being discovered by their current employer.

The other side of the equation is the talent acquisition champion's preference. Some operators are very comfortable cold-calling people, while others prefer the discretion and safety of an email ping. Sometimes comfort with multiple reach-outs, at the expense of feeling like one is being a nuisance, is necessary before some of the targeted folks circle back. This can be due to personal style, preferences, or simply because top talent is usually quite busy. Whatever the case, this is the tedious part of market making that must be done to build an initial pool.

Create a Viable Candidate Pool

Once some of the targeted folks respond, the next conversation (or two) will likely determine which folks the company is interested in, which of them are interested in the company, and whether their interest is high enough for them to apply for the job. Remember, at this point they are not yet candidates, as they have not formally put their names into the hat. All the company is hoping to achieve through this market-making phase is to get enough people who are highly qualified (on paper and based on an initial conversation), interested in the job, and willing to formally submit their resume for review. This pool of people will be combined with those who apply for the job through the platforms or channels where the position has been advertised.

The benefit of proactively making your market is that you don't have to wait for them to reach out to you via traditional channels. The other benefit is that you get to test the level of candidate interest in both the role being offered and the company itself. By doing this groundwork, you can proactively tweak or manage the opportunity to increase the interest levels and calibrate to the market's needs. For example, you may find that some of your requirements for years of experience, technical expertise, or geographic location are not well received by many of the candidates. By having this knowledge earlier in the process, you can choose to revisit your "must haves" versus "nice to haves" and adjust before too much time and energy is spent looking or waiting for folks to respond to the job posting. The other major benefit of attacking the market proactively is that you may realize the level of supply shortage in the market and can calibrate how quickly you can bring someone on board. That has downstream implications on when you can expect to see the financial and operational gains underwritten in your strategy because of this role in your overall human capital plan.

Clearly, the work required in the heavy-touch model consumes more time and energy on the part of the talent acquisition champion and the company, especially if you are looking to fill many positions. If you lack the capacity or capabilities, you may revisit the strategic choice of partnering with a recruiting firm that can build the market for you.

The other key value difference between the two models is *quality* of the candidate pool. A light-touch model tends to lead to a more reactive form of engagement. While it could lead to good talent showing interest in the opportunity, there is a higher probability that there will also be more underqualified applicants. This also creates a major time sink due to a higher volume of underqualified resumes needing to be reviewed. In a tight talent market, with a limited number of qualified candidates, this can cause process delays leading to loss of potential talent to competition. However, with the proactive heavy-touch model, the talent acquisition champion can do a lot of quality control up front by doing a deeper level of diligence before reaching out to potential candidates. This will create a better quality of candidate pool that enters the Talent Acquisition Funnel.

The Candidate's Perspective

All the diligence attributes during this step are equally important for the candidates seeking a job. These attributes manifest themselves in various ways from the candidate's point of view, especially in this early market-making phase, where they still know little about the company, job, and perhaps their own professional needs and plans. A helpful aspect of clear subsegmentation on the company's part is that candidates who are clearly uninterested will likely opt out of the running early in the process. This, in turn, allows your company to have a more refined, qualified pool of candidates to pick from and to only invite interested parties to submit their resumes for reviews.

KEY TAKEAWAYS

- ✓ You can choose to build the market with a light-touch model, which is a bit more passive in its engagement with the market, or a heavier-touch model that requires more active market building.

- ✓ The light-touch model needs a longer runway, given the passive nature of the model, where you are predominantly relying on the candidates to reach out and express interest in the role.

- ✓ The heavy-touch model requires more work and drives clarity through talent segmentation; the higher the clarity on your target, the higher the quality of market you will develop.

CHAPTER 8

ANALYZE RESUMES

DO YOU FIND YOURSELF INTERVIEWING too many unqualified or bad candidates? Do you discover, within the first five minutes of an interview, that it is going to be a waste of time? Are you so busy interviewing that you run out of capacity to do anything else in your day? Do you find a huge disparity between the skills you thought the candidate had and what they are capable of after they started working for you? If the answer to any of these questions is yes, then your company will benefit from the capability to quickly filter out those candidates whose resumes were never good enough to get a meeting invite in the first place. Resume review is a critical step in narrowing down the list of interested applicants to those who might be best for the role, and efficiency in this step will increase the velocity through the Talent Acquisition Funnel. While it may seem like an easy enough task, this candidate due-diligence skill improves with more experience and time. At the simplest level, resumes are chronologically structured statements designed to reveal an applicant's experience, but they can reveal a lot more than most people think. A thorough review allows the recruiting team to be more efficient with its process and significantly improve candidate yield.

The Contents of a Resume

Going back to the foundational principle of spending less time with more, and more time with less, resume review starts with having a clear, diligent, and structured up-front process such that despite speed, you maintain the quality of your process. To calibrate the content, you should focus on the major elements of a resume: the candidate's experience, the consistency of their previous roles, their successes, and their communication style. Between the lines of a resume, you can also find indications of the candidate's ego and can be on the lookout for other red flags.

EXPERIENCE

The purpose of reviewing a resume is to see how closely a candidate's experience aligns with your company's requirements. While it is impractical in this book to highlight nuances for every role, some of the things I spot-check when reviewing resumes for experience include the title and level of responsibility, the size and industry of their previous employers, their role as a player or a coach, and their department or function.

How many times has the candidate had the same title or equivalent responsibility in their past? This tells you if you are going to get a seasoned employee or if the job being offered is their path to graduating into that role. For example, when you need a CEO, you should be looking for someone who has held the titles of CEO, president, or GM. If no such titles are present on their resume, you are less likely to want to speak to them right away. That doesn't mean they are out of the running completely; it just means that they haven't made it to the top of the list yet.

Are candidates coming from businesses of similar size (represented by revenue, EBITDA, the number of customers, or the number of FTEs) to yours, or is the size vastly different? Those coming from larger organizations bring the benefit of scaled operations and processes, while applicants from smaller businesses understand the pain points of similarly sized businesses.

The candidate's current role, coupled with the size of the organizations they are coming from, can be helpful in predicting whether they are willing to get their hands dirty as a player or whether they prefer to manage a larger team as a coach. This also has to dovetail with the current needs of your organization, depending on whether your strategy and team would benefit from a player or coach.

When looking for functional leaders or department heads, it is easy to spot them based on their titles or previous tenures in those categories. The same information can also be very handy in case you are looking to fill a strategically more senior role, such as a GM, but one who has had a functional spike such as sales, marketing, finance, or operations.

CONSISTENCY

You can quickly determine if a candidate has consistently operated at a certain responsibility level or function from an initial scan of their resume. The level of stickiness versus bounciness can be a leading indicator of how the candidate has approached their career.

Seeing a few stints where they have been at a company for three to four years (or more) can be a good indicator of stickiness. It could mean that they are likely to stay with their next employer for the medium term, to benefit from upskilling on the job via coaching or mentoring, and to play a role in bringing stability to the team or culture by not moving quickly.

If they have bounced across a lot of companies (for example, four or five times in ten years), then there is a good chance they will want to fly again. In some instances, such movements can be positive indicators: They may be in high demand because of a unique skill set, or they are both capable and ambitious. On the other hand, it could also mean that they get bored quickly or that they get transitioned out quickly because of poor performance or fit. In some cases, there may be natural reasons for them to move on. These include sale of the company or macro forces or financial crises or personal family reasons. The point is, if you decide to interview the candidate, then you should discuss such movements to better understand their context and drivers. One simple question can be "You have moved a lot in the past ten years. Could you share what led you to those moves and why this job might be a place you could stick around for longer?"

The flip side of this is the case where someone has been in one company for over 80 percent of their professional career. Retention may not be the issue here. The downside is that they have not had the benefit of comparing the processes and cultures of other companies. A change at this time can be difficult for such folks to adjust to. Once again, it's worth the question: "It's great that you have been in one place for so long. Why the change now, and how do you think you will adapt to a different culture?" Another question can be, "Did you not want to explore other businesses, cultures, or organizations?"

SUCCESS

Obviously, we all want to bring a successful person on our team who can contribute or lead the performance improvement of the function, department, or company. So, what are some key success items that are visible on a resume?

Every time the candidate changed jobs, did they get more responsibility, get a bigger title (while not guaranteed, it can be a proxy for more responsibility), or move into a bigger company or division? Did they accelerate their progression within the organization? To me, this is a bigger indicator of success because it can reflect their technical skills, leadership capability, and a political or strategic muscle where necessary (often the case in larger organizations). Depending on your context and strategy, some questions to consider at this stage include: Is there any indication that they were able to effect change and yield quantifiable gains in their previous organizations: higher revenues, lower COGS, improved process efficiencies, increased market share, increased EBITDA, improved enterprise value? Do they have experience with M&A, increasing effectiveness of sales and marketing campaigns, leading organizational design and change work, or integrating acquisitions? Finally, do they demonstrate success outside their work environment, such as leadership roles in the community, participation in sports, other cocurricular achievements, or even personal milestones (assuming they share that in their resume)? Often, these types of engagements can be a good indicator of a well-rounded and interesting person who can add multiple dimensions to your organization and its culture.

COMMUNICATION STYLE

A resume is the first piece of written documentation a candidate shares with the world, and you must believe that this is something they take pride in and where they would want to communicate their experience as clearly as possible. Therefore, a resume should be a good indicator of their communication skills. There are five features in a resume that help me get a sense for a candidate's communication skills.

First, I look for clarity and structure. The clarity with which the candidate has articulated and organized their experience, including bridging roles, titles, years, and experiences can reveal how they think and communicate. If the resume is unstructured, there is a good chance this person will produce work that will be similarly chaotic. If the talent acquisition champion or hiring manager is very structured in their thinking and problem-solving, such a resume will not appeal to them.

Next, I look for brevity. A tightly written resume that is succinct and prioritized can be a great indicator of the kind of person who is likely to show up at the interview. If it is too short and appears incomplete or too long describing experiences in unnecessary detail, that could raise a red flag. While not a disqualifier in and of itself, it is an insightful data point to be captured at this point in your review.

I also notice their attention to detail. Are all the facts on the page and stated precisely? I start by looking for two things. First, do they have all the dates for each of their jobs? Any missing dates or overlapping dates that don't make sense give me pause. Second, within the list of quantitative achievements, do they use precise numbers to highlight the outcomes? A lack of such data can often suggest a less detail-oriented individual. My general rule is, look for precision in a resume and ask for depth in an interview.

I scan for errors. While this is technically a subset of attention to detail, it deserves its own spot. An error-free resume is not a major hurdle these days, especially with spell-check tools that candidates can access, such as Grammarly, Resume Worded, and ChatGPT. Therefore, a resume with errors indicates that the candidate does not have sufficient attention to detail, does not care enough about their market reputation, or simply has bad communication practices. None of these makes me want to schedule a live interview.

I look at the candidate's breadth of experience: The primary goal is to find top talent for job specifications, especially for technical roles such as finance or technology. However, it is often good to have folks within the company who have a more well-rounded or broader skill set. Breadth of experience can come from working at different scales (ranging from Fortune 500 to start-ups), across industries, geographies, or cultures, or from developing tools outside the work environment (such as in the military or sports) that could help in the business world.

EGO

While a resume should be about the person, someone with awareness of their ego can separate themselves from those who struggle to do so. People with higher levels of self-awareness and emotional intelligence tend to use the words *we* or *the company* in their resumes to highlight achievements. Consequently, their resume will strike the right balance between demonstration of achievements and self-promotion. Engagement in team sports and community work can be additional indicators of someone who might be a good team player. On the contrary, if you see resumes with lots of "I" at the start of each sentence, during an interview you should evaluate how much of their ego plays into how they manage or work alongside team members.

RED FLAGS

The resume can indicate obvious red and yellow flags that help me eliminate resumes from the interview pool. For example, a lack of fit between the role and their experience. We have all received resumes where folks have done a mass distribution without even getting the company name correct, let alone explaining how their background makes sense for the job.

Constant company hopping (for instance, more than five companies in ten years) is a surefire way for many candidates to make it into my do-not-interview pile. Major gaps in work experience are the same. Resumes with large periods of time away from work are a yellow flag at minimum. There are of course legitimate reasons, such as family and health, for people to step away from work. But outside of those understandable reasons, it becomes tricky for those who have not had consistency in work to compete with others who have.

Processing Resumes

Finally, let me share with you the process and timeline that you must devote to resume reviews. After all, our primary goal here is to be efficient and to start talking to people ASAP. Without moving forward, resume reviews are nothing more than an academic exercise.

Identify resumes to be put into three tiers (see figure 8.1) with an initial scan. A tier 1 candidate's fit is great across most—if not all—requirements for the job being filled, with no obvious flags. The talent acquisition champion or hiring manager must speak to them ASAP. They are the closest to the bull's-eye, at least theoretically. Tier 2 is not an obvious fit, but if tier 1 folks don't do well in their interviews, you can quickly talk to folks in tier 2. The minimum criteria for someone in this tier is some experiential requirements. You may choose to let go of industry or other needs, but if they cannot do the job, they are moved to tier 3, where they are turned

Fit criteria	Tier 1	Tier 2	Tier 3	
Industry fit (where required)	✓	?	?	✗
Experience fit Seniority/titles Roles and responsibilities Achievements/success Types of initiatives and deliverables People management	✓	✓	?	✗
Other Consistency and commitment Communication style Self-awareness (ego/empathy) Nonprofessional engagements	✓	?	?	✗

✓ Meets requirements   ? Meets some but not all requirements   ✗ Does not meet requirement

Figure 8.1   Resume tiering structure

down. There is no need to speak to this last tier, and you will want to avoid having such resumes in the pipeline. These are resumes with yellow and red flags across all components of fit or criteria. There is absolutely no need for anyone in the company to waste their own time or the candidate's when it comes to filling the role. Save it by focusing on tiers 1 and 2.

Our goal here is to quickly identify tier 3 resumes and reduce sources of such inflow. This will require you to realign on your channel strategy. For example, if you are using an online channel (e.g., LinkedIn), make direct edits in the job description or requirements to remove terms or add traits that can reduce the flow of tier 3 applicants. If you are using a recruiting partner, then proactively give them quick feedback to ensure they have your clear views on what you like and dislike so they can stop the follow of tier 3 candidates.

Don't accumulate. One of the biggest mistakes CEOs make is that they wait for resumes to reach a critical mass before they review the pile. This can either be a preferred practice or a result of insufficient capacity. Either way, this approach often backfires. First, candidates are not going to wait too long for the company to get in touch. Remember, you and your hiring team are not the only game in town, and it is possible that you may need the talent more than they need the job. Second, waiting will diminish your enterprise value without filling open roles, especially as they tie back to growth strategy. The longer you wait to figure out how far the supply side is from the bull's-eye candidate profile, the more difficult it will be to recalibrate your unmet organizational needs. Also, the quicker the talent acquisition champion can get your feedback to tweak the job description, experience requirements, or channel strategy, the quicker you will see an improvement in the quality of inbound resumes.

Finally, although it is still early in the execution phase, *move quickly*! There is a lot to do to get through the TAF, which means there is absolutely no time to waste. The sooner you get cracking, the sooner you will have top talent join the organization, and the sooner value creation can start.

To facilitate consistently high speed to action, it is important for the talent acquisition champion and hiring team to schedule a dedicated weekly meeting or call with key company stakeholders or recruiting partners. It does not mean that you cannot provide feedback or make changes sooner than a week. It means that since you need to run the business while building your teams, you and your acquisition team may otherwise simply run out of mental or calendar runway. This weekly block reserves the necessary time to ensure that talent acquisition continues to be your top priority.

We are talking minutes, not hours for the tiering process—thirty to forty-five minutes per week. It should take a couple of minutes per resume. On a good week, around five to seven resumes may come in for review, which means ten to fifteen minutes total for this process. As illustrated in figure 8.2, a large volume of candidates can be processed quickly at this step, reserving your capacity to spend more time with fewer preferred candidates later in the TAF. If you are getting more than five good-quality resumes each week—amazing! Notwithstanding the quality of those resumes, the volume shows good market-building effort and awareness of the job opening. Feedback to your recruiting partner (if you have one) should also take only five to ten minutes on a call, or jot it down for them in an email. In the event you are running this search in-house, the talent acquisition

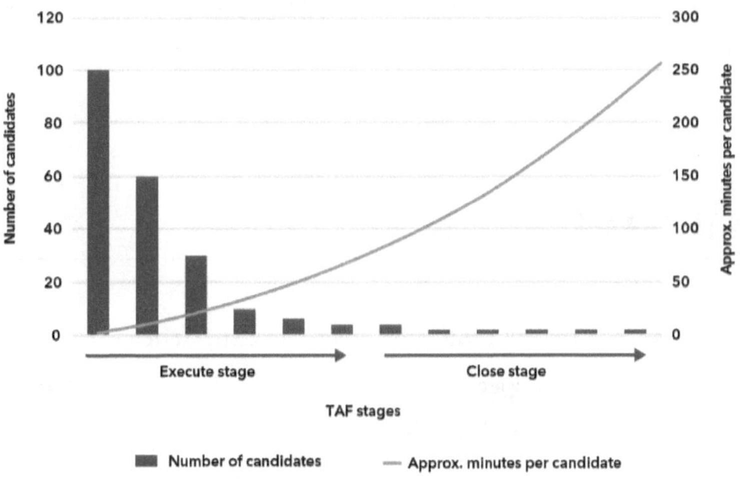

Figure 8.2 The relationship between candidate volume and time per candidate using the Talent Acquisition Funnel

champion can share the feedback and calibrate with the hiring team in approximately the same amount of time.

Eric Biro, Founding Partner of Anderson Biro, a US-based B2B services company that includes an executive search business, explained:

> Slow and steady does not work in this business. In my experience, nearly a third of the time, candidates walk away from a deal because companies have taken too long to engage or come back with an offer. This starts right from the beginning of the process, where I need to review their resumes quickly so I can have the best chance of speaking to those who fit the role before I lose them to my competition.[1]

Finally, edits to the job description or experience requirements should take ten to fifteen minutes maximum. After a couple of early iterations, you will want to freeze changes to allow the market to respond. Continuous tweaking confuses the candidates and will also create procedural chaos for your team.

KEY TAKEAWAYS

- ✓ Resumes reveal a lot more than just experience and highlight specific areas for you to ask some pointed questions during interviews.

- ✓ You can spot red or yellow flags during quick resume scans that disqualify a candidate, saving time and hence creating capacity for yourself and your team.

✓ Organizing resumes into tiers saves the talent acquisition team a lot of time by not speaking with candidates far from the ideal profile.

✓ Allow for a weekly cadence to review resumes and to speak with the recruiting team (internally or third party) to ensure quick recalibration, process consistency, and speed.

CHAPTER 9

LEVERAGE BEHAVIORAL TOOLS

J UST AS WITH ANY WELL-RUN M&A due diligence, the timely use of accurate and relevant data in the talent acquisition process will lead to better-quality and high-speed decision-making. Whether it is the first employee of the company or whether the company already has a triple-digit or more head count, behavioral data tools help triage a large pool of resumes to get to a shortlist of hyperprioritized applicants who deserve to be interviewed. The intention here is to increase the efficiency and effectiveness of the limited capacity, time, and mindshare of the company's executive team to focus on a targeted list of folks who are most likely to succeed in the role.

As Josh Finifter, Managing Director at US-based private equity fund Access Holdings, explained:

The best investments are built on comprehensive data-driven diligence, and the best teams are too. That is why my team and I use third-party tools to complement data collected during interviews. It transforms our people diligence.[1]

The tactical benefit of using these tools is that data and insights from them can reduce the number of tier 2 resumes by either moving them into tier 1 or pushing them into tier 3. The triaging of tier 2 candidates allows the hiring team to utilize the saved time to invest in a richer diligence on a select few candidates or toward running the day-to-day business.

These tools also enable the talent acquisition champion and the hiring team to better assess each candidate's potential across attributes such as their attention to detail or sense of urgency relative to the needs of the job. Also, the data can shed some light on individual elements such as social ability and empathy and relative fit with the existing culture within the organization.

While most tools require a nominal up-front investment, both the efficiency gain and the quicker job fulfillment, leading to required throughput from the role, result in accelerated value creation for the company and better ROI for the business. At a minimum, you save an incredible number of hours from not interviewing bad candidates combined with the prevention of tremendous value destruction from making a bad hire.

When it comes to using such tools, I suggest companies should use something—anything. It is more important to boost your team's capability than to get a perfect tool, which does not exist anyway. Simply start using something to collect incremental data that turbo-charges your people diligence process. They key principle to be mindful of is that these tools are informative instruments that help you pressure-test or build on your hypotheses from resume reviews or in-person interviews. There is no substitute for a resume review that leverages the experience and skills of the hiring manager to compare against the technical and experiential fit of the candidate. If you haven't reviewed any resumes or spoken to the candidate, then these tools should not be used in a vacuum to make the decisions for you. Finally, the key to success with these tools is being consistent about using them to cumulatively capitalize on saved time, energy, and cost, as well as poor talent quality and quantity. The biggest advocate for consistency must be the CEO or the talent acquisition champion; if you don't push for it, no one else will.

There are plenty of additional tools in the market beyond those discussed here. My suggestion is to find one that you find insightful and your hiring team likes, can afford, and will use most frequently. Lock it in, and start using it. If after a few years you want to switch to a different tool, do so. But get something—anything—into the organization and start leveraging it to save time and cost and hire the right people for your company or at a minimum avoid hiring the wrong people.

The Culture Index and Predictive Index are psychometric tools that help assess a candidate's overall personality across multiple categories and can be calibrated to the characteristics required for the role's success. They also provide insight into a candidate's understanding of what it would take for them to be successful in their job and how far they would need to deviate from their natural traits to do so.

The Myers–Briggs Type Indicator (MBTI) and DiSC system are another category of products that some companies use to best understand the personalities and behavioral preferences of their employees. This helps leaders facilitate better working relationships between their employees. These tools can inform hiring decisions by identifying a candidate's fit relative to the profile of the incumbent team.

People Quotient's leadership due diligence application is hyperfocused on delivering an executive operating profile of C-suite executives to middle managers. It allows CEOs, investors, and leaders in an organization to get to know their people by assessing tangible leadership capabilities across key operational pillars and tactical traits. It provides detailed insights at the individual level but also highlights patterns across a cohort of leaders both within a company and across organizations. Insights from the tool allow leaders to be able to take definitive action for incumbent leadership teams, as well as during talent acquisition, to ultimately build high-performing management teams.

One of the incremental benefits of these tools can be insights on the EQ levels of the candidates. While most of the tools have indicators that can suggest EQ levels directionally (e.g., Feeling versus Thinking in MBTI; Logic score in the Culture Index), People Quotient's product tends to address their operational implications.

Pam Vona, CEO and Cofounder of a US-based B2B services business, shared her experience with use of data-driven tools to augment her talent diligence process:

> Gut instinct is an important part of decision-making and can often provide valuable insights. However, as people, we are all fallible and can easily misinterpret things based on biases, emotions, or limited perspective. That's why I've found psychometric evaluations and other third-party data tools to be such incredible resources in the hiring process. They help validate—or challenge—my initial impressions and ensure I'm making more objective, well-rounded decisions. Using these tools has both saved me time by filtering out candidates who weren't the right fit and spared my company from the setbacks of bad hires. As a small business owner, combining gut instinct with data-driven tools has been a game changer for me and my team.[2]

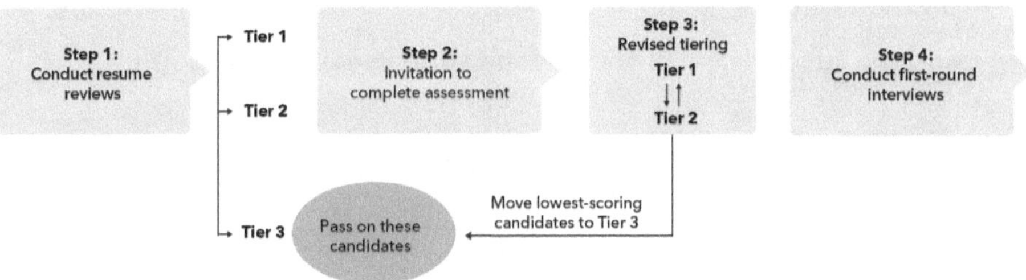

Figure 9.1   Resume triaging and leveraging assessments and tools

You can follow a simple process (see figure 9.1) for using behavioral tools in talent acquisition. First, review resumes and put your candidates into the three tiers. For tier 1 and tier 2 resume candidates only, send the request to complete one of the tools-based assessment surveys (e.g., People Quotient's PQ5, DiSC, MBTI, Culture Index, or Predictive Index). No point sending anything to tier 3 candidates. If they are not qualified to begin with, any additional energy from you will be wasteful and is best used for the other tiers. Next, use the survey results to decide if any of the tier 2 candidates should move into tier 1 or vice versa. Finally, invite candidates for their first interview. Using the assessment tools as a gating item—that is, refusing to speak to candidates who have not completed them, no matter how good their resume—increases your capacity and effectiveness, which forces adoption both internally and externally.

One additional benefit of such tools is that you can use these to better understand your existing employee base as well as the organizational interplay. Leveraging the tool that works best for your company creates a unifying language with which teammates understand each other better, managers can coach the teams better, and talent acquisition can become laser focused in adding the right people on the team. All of this will positively affect the company's culture and the effectiveness of your organization as you continue to scale.

KEY TAKEAWAYS

- ✓ Use data-driven tools. They give a company more insight not only so it can get to the short list of ideal candidates but also so it can get there more quickly.

- ✓ Consistent use of these tools gives your company a richer and comparable dataset over time, as well as more insights into the real-life accuracy of the tool.

- ✓ There are no perfect tools. You just need to pick one (by either trial and error or asking around), and use it to provide additional insights you would not have otherwise gained only from a resume review.

- ✓ Leverage the tools beyond talent acquisition to learn about your existing employees and how their individual traits may influence the company culture.

CHAPTER 10

ROUND 1 INTERVIEWS

Interviewing candidates is a great privilege and mutual
exchange. We need to remember that we've all been on the
other side of the table and need to treat candidates with care
and respect because interviews can be very stressful. First interviews
are two-way sales conversations, where both parties have a short
window to make great first impressions. Great candidates have
options, so as much as they need to impress me, I also need
to impress them and sell them on joining our team.

—ISRAEL NIEZEN, CEO at Factored, USA and Colombia[1]

GOING BACK TO THE TALENT ACQUISITION FUNNEL'S operating
principle of being clinical in your diligence and eliminating
subpar candidates fast, take the opportunity of the first interview
to spend time with tier 1 (and if needed, tier 2) candidates to be
able to decide who should move further through the funnel. The
purpose of the first round of interviews is twofold: First, who has
the potential for getting the job and is therefore worth further

investment of the rest of the team's capability and capacity in the next few rounds? This is not the time to make a hiring decision. The goal is simply to determine who gets to move forward. That's it! Second, determine who is clearly someone the team does not wish to move forward. By removing these candidates from the process, you will save capability and capacity to apply to those who have moved to the next round.

Prepare for the Interview

Remember, an interview is also a selling and marketing round. Candidates will react to the company's level of preparedness, excitement, and professionalism at this point and through the rest of the TAF. A lack of a structure will not only lead to poor diligence; it can also lead to reputational damage if the candidates experience an unstructured and poor discussion with you.

As Nancy Splaine, Founder and CEO of Connecting Point Marketing Group, USA, noted:

> Interviewing is a two-way dialogue. Not only are you interviewing the candidate, but they are also interviewing you and assessing if you are or the organization is the right fit for them. Be open-minded and be kind. You will learn the values of the person you are interviewing and vice versa.[2]

Some companies and hiring managers try to improvise their first-round interviews. Beyond the potential impression this leaves on your candidates, it is also inefficient and leads to poor outcomes. The interviewers either move too many applicants forward, meaning the next round will consume a large portion of the company's capability and capacity, or terminate good candidates too soon because the questions were not thoughtful enough.

You must *prepare*. Their resume should already be familiar from the reviews during the tiering process and before any invitations to complete the behavioral tool were sent to the candidates. You should also have results from the screening tool to help you identify areas of the candidate's personality or behavior that you will explore during the interview. For instance, is their attention to detail a fit for the role and your company? Are they likely to be more task oriented or do you need a big-picture thinker in this role? Are they likely to have lower EQ than the job and the company requires?

Finally, make sure your questions are consistent. A handful of (usually around three) standardized questions across candidates is a useful way of comparing a diverse pool of applicants. Of course, you should have more job-specific diligence questions, but by limiting to three or fewer standardized questions, the conversation gets a chance to breathe, letting you evaluate the candidate's unique experiences and allowing an organic interaction between the parties.

ASSESSING CANDIDATES' EQ LEVELS

One of the major benefits of an interview is that you can begin to assess the candidate's EQ needs relative to what you will have identified using the EQ Matrix when you defined the role. Table 10.1 outlines where and how candidate EQ levels can be determined during the first round of interviews and as an input into the EQ Deep Dive Framework in subsequent interview rounds.

continued →

TABLE 10.1. INTERVIEW DATA POINTS TO EVALUATE CANDIDATE'S EQ LEVELS

Context	EQ attribute or trait	Observations and data points on EQ levels
Pre-interview interactions with broader team	1. Empathy/kindness 2. Respect 3. Thoughtfulness	Admin team feedback is incredibly useful in continuing to assess a candidate's EQ levels. Some examples: 1. Level of ease or difficulty to work with them to schedule interviews and to submit resumes and other background info. 2. Demonstration of respect and kindness during phone conversations, in voicemails, and in written correspondence 3. Specific data points indicating candidate's thoughtfulness, such as in-person etiquette, respectful interest in the team, and demonstrating interest in the position/opportunity without being pushy
Interactions with the interviewer	1. Respect (vs. rudeness) 2. Listening skills 3. Kindness (vs. aggressiveness) 4. Interpersonal style	This depends a fair amount on an interviewer's ability to ask insightful questions to extract EQ levels (see "Insightful Diligence" section later in chapter). In many cases it is easier to spot situations of low EQ than high EQ. 1. Disrespectful body language or dismissive/unimpressed facial expressions 2. Swearing or harsh language 3. Constant interruption and impatient style of engagement 4. Confrontational style to answering questions

Context	EQ attribute or trait	Observations and data points on EQ levels
Interview content	1. Self-awareness 2. Handling pushback/pressure 3. Collaborative (balance between self and team)	Low-EQ indicators: 1. Exclusive use of "I" versus attribution to team achievements 2. Visible and audible demonstration of frustration and even anger during interview discussion 3. No use of examples of team-based projects or successes
Post-interview interactions with the team	1. Empathy 2. Respect 3. Kindness	1. Proactive, courteous follow-up with the interviewer or hiring team after the interview 2. The act of following up can reveal thoughtful and respectful elements of the candidate and additionally a directional indicator of continued interest. 3. Personalized language that indicates kindness and respect

Structure the Interview

A structure that works, sticking to it, and sharing it with the candidate allows both them and you to know what to expect. The first thirty-five to forty minutes is dedicated to your part. That starts with a brief intro about how you—the interviewer—fit into the interview process as well as the company. But most of this time is dedicated to your own questions for the candidate. Try to make it feel like a conversation rather than an inquisition. Sometimes candidates prefer to just answer questions, as opposed to having a dialogue, in which case it's best to let them feel comfortable and for you to move on with your questions.

On the point of questions, while most of us believe that we ask smart questions, sadly that confidence is grossly misplaced. The most common interview questions—such as asking about their resume; their reasons for applying; and their goals, strengths, and weaknesses—are decent but not the most effective for your diligence: Every candidate knows these questions are coming, they make the conversation boring, and they reveal only basic info on the candidate. It's better to take an alternative approach with which you can make your questions a lot more insightful. Your questions should push the candidates to think a bit harder and reveal a lot more during the interview process, yielding a deeper and richer dataset about the candidate. To complement the alternative questions (see table 10.2), I use data from the resume review and screening tools to dig a bit deeper into areas where I see potential red or yellow flags.

Allow twenty to twenty-five minutes for them to ask you questions. While it may seem that they have less time to talk than you do, in a more conversational interview, it is likely that you have been answering some of their questions along the way. The idea of this dedicated time is to make sure they know that they will have time to ask as many questions as they want at the end. This way, they won't feel rushed or worried that they will walk away from the first interview not knowing much more than when they came in.

Pay attention to the number of questions they ask and how thoughtful those questions are. If they don't ask any questions throughout or at the end during their dedicated time, it is usually a major red flag that indicates that they were unprepared or that they are simply uninterested. In my estimation, this amounts to a turndown, and they are likely not going to work out in the job anyway. You want people to be excited to join your company and curious about their role. Given nerves and excitement, their questions may be simple and standard; however, those who ask me insightful and thoughtful questions tend to distinguish themselves from the rest of the pack.

On your side of the table, I strongly encourage you to be as transparent in your responses as possible. The candidates are flying partially blind; until now, the only sense of the company and the job likely came from online research, discussions with recruiters (if one was involved), and the job description. This initial conversation is the first live discussion they are going to have with someone from the company. I recognize that in some cases, there will be a need to sign NDAs to share confidential information and substantive data with candidates. But other than that, the more honest you are, the more accurately you can evaluate candidate reactions and be assured that your future interest is well informed. Attracting candidates with limited or, worse, nonfactual data is always going to get a company into longer-term trouble with the employees. Would you want to be led on to make one of the most important professional decisions of your life?

For the last few minutes, as you wrap up, and even if the interview is running over, take a couple of minutes to give them a sense of what to expect next: who they will be hearing back from, the next step, and a general timeline of the process. Clarity will speak to the company's ability to run a tight process, which will almost always leave any top talent feeling good about your organization.

As the candidates move through the interview stages, the talent acquisition champion should continue to process applicants via market building, resume analysis, and leveraging behavioral tools to ensure the funnel is consistently being filled by new interviewees, ideally continuing to work through the front end of the funnel until three or four candidates get to the case interview.

Insightful Diligence

Implementing the above strategy and structure simply comes down to asking good, insightful questions. Creative questioning will transform your dataset on the candidates and allow you to get richer diligence on key traits relevant to the role. Most candidates should be well prepared to provide good, quality answers to commonly used, cookie-cutter questions, which limits your ability to separate the good from the best. By asking alternative questions, our intention is not to trick the candidates in any way but to help them explore and articulate their journey through a different lens, allowing you the benefit of understanding their choices, experiences, and learnings. Let's look at a few pairs of commonly used questions and their more insightful counterparts with the intention of inspiring you to develop your own set of alternative questions.

If we start with the topic of understanding their employment history and choices, a typical question would be, *Walk me through your resume.* This is an age-old question that does not reveal much and quite frankly is underwhelming and unimpressive for the candidates to hear. If an interviewer has done their job to prepare for the interview, then they can instead ask, *What is the one thing that you are most proud of (excited about) on your resume?* You can then save ten minutes listening to their rehearsed monologue and instead give yourself a chance dive deeper with follow-up questions, revealing a much more useful dataset. Similarly, instead of asking, *Why are you looking for a job?* or *What are you looking for in it?* or *Why does this job make sense?* or *What are your goals?*, try asking something like: *Help me understand the arc you wish to paint for your career. How does this job fit at this point in your professional journey?* The benefits of this more open-ended approach are simple. First, you get to learn if they have a future vision for their career, which is relevant for most executives and aspiring future leaders. Second, this requires them to bridge their past experiences to their future vision, naturally giving you insights into their employment history. Third, you can assess their ability to communicate a plan, albeit about themselves, and find out if they have done any research on your company and the job at hand to connect the dots.

When investigating a candidate's skills and strengths or weaknesses, an unimaginative set of questions would be *What are your strengths or what are your weaknesses?* While perfectly fine questions, they don't inspire a thoughtful response. Instead, ask, *What is the one thing that is distinctive about you?* Or *What is the one thing that your colleagues always count on you for?* Take the conversation from a laundry list of many traits to focus on one. This also gives you a sense of their self-awareness, an important EQ trait, and if they can prioritize (something otherwise hard to assess in a short conversation).

When it comes to exploring weaknesses, approach with questions such as *What is the one thing you wish you were better at?* Sometimes I ask the question *What do you suck at?* You might try *What would your coach/mentor wish you to improve?* or *What developmental feedback or coaching have you consistently received the most in the last two years?* Many people make up a weakness that sounds good, but when they're asked about something they need to keep developing, they are more willing to reveal the truth about skills they may genuinely struggle with. I specifically ask this to senior executive candidates to explore their self-awareness and to determine if, for strategic or operational reasons, it may not make sense for them to oversee certain departments or functions. You will be surprised how many answer the question truthfully.

Table 10.2 provides a summary of better ways to phrase select common first-round interview questions.

While the topics in the table are covered in most first-round interviews, some critical deep dive categories that often get forgotten include leadership skills, sense of autonomy for self and their teams, sense of urgency and attention to detail, and ability to manage change and prioritize. Having clarity on what you are solving for in each of these categories, as it relates to the job you are trying to fill, will help you identify the specific questions you should be asking.

When it comes to leadership, you may need to assess the candidate's capabilities to have followers or develop other leaders, their

Table 10.2. Sampling of alternative questions for first-round interviews

Category	Standard question	Better question
Employment	Walk me through your resume.	What is the one thing that you are most proud of on your resume?
	Why are you looking for a job?	Help me understand the arc you wish to paint for your career.
Skills and strengths	What are your strengths?	What is the one thing that your colleagues will say they count on you for?
Weaknesses	What are your weaknesses?	What is the one thing you have already been working on that you believe still needs a lot of work?

style of engaging the team, their level of empathy, and so on. Some questions to inspire such diligence include:

- How do they balance between prescriptive and descriptive approaches to helping their teams?

- What is their track record on people retention, promotion, and voluntary attrition?

- How would their direct reports or peers describe their experience of the interviewee's leadership?

On the topic of autonomy, you may choose to evaluate the leader's preference for autonomy for self as well as for those they manage. As examples, a couple of my favorite creative questions that explore this are:

- If I were on their team, would I get to design and implement processes or would I have to follow their approach?

- On a scale of 0 to 5 where 5 is a highly autonomous operator and leader, what score would they get from a $360°$ feedback review?

If having a sense of urgency or attention to detail are necessary traits to be successful in the role, then your interview questions complemented with data from the behavioral tools can be a very powerful way to evaluate such a skill set. Explore by using questions such as:

- What is the upper limit of number of projects they can successfully handle and enjoy at a time?

- What number of transformational projects did they lead in their last role and within what time frame?

- How did they measure and track progress using metrics such as revenue, growth rates, COGS, EBITDA, margins, and head counts in those transformational projects?

One of the key skills most jobs require, particularly for senior roles, is to manage change and ruthlessly prioritize issues. Examples of questions to explore the candidate's approach to prioritization include:

- Describe your biggest struggle during implementation of a tough change initiative and how you navigated that.
- What is your primary metric for prioritizing your and your team's focus?
- Describe when and why you stopped or paused a major project to prioritize another initiative in the business.

The above questions are designed to take the traditional interview diligence approach of identifying the *what* a candidate may have accomplished in their career and move toward truly trying to understand the *why* and *how* behind those events. This increases both the efficiency of the interviews and the effectiveness of your process. It will allow you to eliminate underqualified candidates earlier from the Talent Acquisition Funnel and improve the quality of the candidate pool entering the next few steps in the funnel.

Interview with Excitement, Not Ego

I have seen folks from all sides of the table lean heavily on the might of their ego while engaging with talent. I am particularly passionate about this topic because I have seen great candidates walk away because of the interviewer's ego. Similarly, I have seen candidates full to the brim with ego who have made it easy for employers to walk away from them. Bringing awareness to this topic can help you course correct quickly and increase your talent acquisition yield.

As Ankit Shah, President of a US-based sports cardiology business, noted:

> When I talk to the candidates for the first time, I try to remind myself that I must impress them too. As a small business owner, you are the poster child for your business. Your excitement will come naturally from within and will always show, but ego is manufactured and easy to spot by those you interview. The difference is night and day. Let your passion, not ego, lead the process.[3]

The best way to interview or acquire talent is with excitement. If you are not excited, then you need to stop and rethink how you want to build your team. No one wants to join a team where the hiring manager is not excited to fill the role. But don't fake it; your disingenuousness will be found out either in the recruiting process or when the talent joins, and the lack of integrity will eventually lead them to quit and put you right back where you started.

Remember, your excitement can be infectious and separate you from the fierce competition for top talent. Whether you are interviewing a CEO candidate, level 2s reporting to the CEO, or other folks in the organization, knowing that you may not be the only game in town, it is essential that you bring your A game and a selling mindset, or else you will lose. Approach the conversation genuinely wanting to learn about this person. This mindset starts during the first step of resume review when you find the initial read makes you want to speak to the candidate. Your honest desire to get to know the person comes through in your body language, your choice of words, and your tone.

A mistaken approach is when I see some hiring managers try to impress candidates by asking tough "gotcha" questions that don't serve a true purpose in revealing the candidates' skills or gaps relative to the needs of the job. These tactics can be dilutive to your purpose of trying to present a healthy and collegial future team environment. Such tactics may serve the interviewer's ego but lose great talent. It's also good to remember that not everyone you interview is desperate for a job. If anything, almost certainly a large proportion of the people you are interviewing currently have a job. The only facts you can trust are that there is a gap in your organization, how desperately (or not) you need the role filled, and the loss in enterprise value each day you don't have someone in that seat. You should be just as excited about the candidate's interest in your company as they are in joining it. This excitement can be infectious; if you are excited about them, then there is a good chance they will get excited about you and the role. After all, who doesn't want to be somewhere or with someone who is excited to hear their story? And if they don't get pumped despite your excitement, then you probably don't have the right match anyway.

Another thing I remind CEOs is that while you may hold the purse strings for the job in your company, you are not the only buyer. You are there to purchase the candidate's talent, and they are there to purchase your vision for the company, department, or team. You are both a seller and a buyer here. I am not discounting the fact that, as the hiring company, you are going to pay a market—or above market—price for the work or that you may have a slight upper hand if you have other choices of talented candidates. But your goal is to not make this entire experience one-sided. Remember, you both want something awesome out of this experience, so treat your candidates like they are as much of a buyer as you are. A few subtle ways of bringing the candidate into the fold while also highlighting good operating values of your organization comes from the language you use throughout the interview process. This means choosing more "we" than "I," or "us" rather than "me" when describing your company's culture and accomplishments.

Your candidates are looking to buy and you should be excited to sell the following elements of your company:

- Vision: Your conviction in where your company should be heading, how it will get there, and how the role they are interviewing for fits within that journey and destination.

- Security: The job is secure, the company is on stable footing, and the company or department will be there for many years to come.

- Culture: Their only window into the culture of the company is through the handful of conversations with you and the others throughout the hiring process. They need to believe—and so buy—that you and your team are consistent and genuine. The worst thing you can do as an interviewer or hiring team is present the values of teamwork, empathy, and support and yet during the interview process, consciously or otherwise, demonstrate polar opposite behaviors. There is never any need or place for such behaviors. While this may end up helping the candidates recognize a major issue, resulting in them withdrawing from the process, it ultimately affects your company's talent acquisition capability and stifles its growth.

- Values: Your values become obvious in your actions and how you treat the candidates, not just by talking about those values. For example, if one of your values is respect, then treat the candidate with respect. If it is honesty, don't use fake numbers or lie during the process, just as you want the same from them.

- Headroom: They want to know that as the company grows or other possibilities arise within the organization, there will be true opportunities for them to grow and to be compensated accordingly.

Another counsel I share with CEOs and hiring managers is that it is important for you to imagine how excited and nervous that person would be coming to the interview. They have probably been thinking about and preparing for this interview for days, likely had an anxious sleep the night before, and woke up to get dressed and put their best game face on while also dealing with life at home and their current job, and perhaps a lot is riding on this job. That excitement is what they are bringing to this meeting. As the interviewer, you can honor all of that by trying to learn about who they are both as a professional and as a person.

KEY TAKEAWAYS

✓ Never show up to the interview without processing all the candidate data from the prior steps, including insights from the resume and behavioral tool.

✓ Make this into a dialogue; ask questions that give you insights—not information—about the candidate.

✓ Remember, their questions can shed light on their preparedness, thinking process, and interest in the company and role.

✓ Always finish the interview with clarity about the process and the next steps.

✓ Be mindful that you are not the only game in town. Assume that good talent always has options. You may need them more than they need you.

✓ Remember, they are also a buyer at the table; curbing your ego and embracing genuine excitement will show through. The candidates are buyers of your vision, leadership style, company culture, and the importance of the role. You need to sell too!

✓ The honest intention to learn about the candidate will lead to a more fulsome experience for them and exhaustive diligence for you.

CHAPTER 11

FOLLOW-UP INTERVIEWS

We all have stories to tell, and during a series of
interviews one of the key pieces of a good hiring team
is to piece together the stories of each candidate to best
understand who they are. It's the job of the person leading the
process to make sure that happens and it happens consistently.

—**MARK SINATRA**, CEO of Aspen HR, USA,
and eight-time Inc. 5000 CEO[1]

EMPLOYERS RARELY HIRE ANYONE after just one conversation. The main aim of additional interviews is to collect additional insights on each candidate, ensuring robust diligence before moving them to the final round: the case discussion. At the end of the first round, you should be able to put the candidates into one of two buckets. Either you move them forward because you see a cultural fit, they are qualified for the job, and investing more time and energy into their candidacy is the right thing to do. Or they do not have the right set of skills and traits and therefore should be excused from the process. That's it.

For the candidates in the latter bucket, you should communicate their exclusion from the process quickly, candidly, succinctly, and with kindness. For those who are in the qualified bucket, your goal is to build a comprehensive thesis to determine who gets on the short list and eventually to the offer stage as they pass through the acquisition funnel.

In the follow-up rounds, you first need to have a clear sense of *what*. With additional conversations, we are trying to build a clearer story for each of the candidates, and specifically clarity on a few key items will help you accelerate the right candidates through the Talent Acquisition Funnel. It starts with each interviewer, if you have more than one on your team, being clear on each candidate's rank relative to others in the pool. It is best that the interviewers don't broadcast candidates' rankings to other colleagues involved in the interviewing process to avoid group think and bias. However, it is critical that you share with the rest of the hiring team the set of attributes you like, including those that you wish for them to pressure-test further. Being specific on these items is most helpful, whether it's analytics, strategy, emotional intelligence, technical skills, or any other capabilities relevant to the role. Finally, just as in the first round, a handful of consistent questions that each interviewer asks is helpful, to allow the hiring team to compare and calibrate across the slate of candidates.

EMOTIONAL INTELLIGENCE: A DEEP DIVE

Follow-up interviews are a perfect opportunity for CEOs and their hiring teams to do diligence on the emotional intelligence (EQ) of a short list of candidates. Earlier in the Talent Acquisition Funnel, you will have leveraged the EQ Matrix to identify levels of EQ required to be successful in the company and this role. Also, by this stage of the process, you will have had several opportunities to collect data on the emotional intelligence of this pool of candidates. This includes their written and verbal communication content and style; their experiences both in the job and outside; their approach to interacting with people at the company including assistants, associates, managers, and executives alike; and their behavior throughout the funnel steps, particularly when they are pushed on their answers during round 1 of the interviews.

According to Nancy Splaine, Founder and CEO of Connecting Point Marketing Group, USA, and a seasoned private equity operator and advisor:

> EQ shows up everywhere during the interview process. One of my favorite things is to find out how the candidate greeted my employees when they met, if the candidate was kind and thoughtful throughout the process or if they had arrogance or rudeness at any point in time. There is no one question that you can ask to figure out emotional intelligence. It's in almost everything we do.[2]

In key managerial and executive roles, you should dedicate a reasonable amount of time in one of the follow-up interviews, ideally led by a high-EQ person on your team, to focus on EQ diligence. Use the simple four-step EQ Deep Dive Framework shown in figure 11.1 to diagnose and understand the capabilities of each of the candidates. The intention here is not so much to evaluate what happened (unless the outcome is directly relevant to the purpose of the position/role) but to focus more on how it was handled by the candidate and how it may or may not have changed them— their philosophies, principles, or practices.

continued →

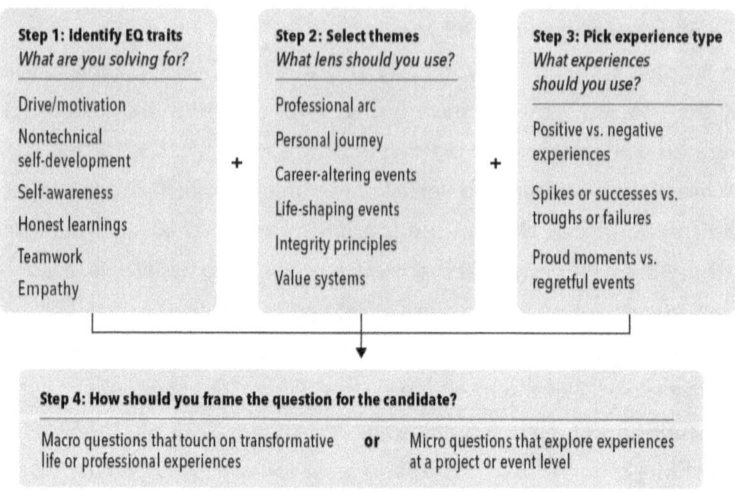

Figure 11.1   EQ Deep Dive Framework

STEP 1: IDENTIFY REQUIRED EQ TRAITS

Identify the specific EQ traits such as empathy, motivation, self-awareness, drive, and any others that will make the employee successful in the company and this role.

STEP 2: SELECT THEMES

It is always better to have the candidate self-select a theme such as their professional arc, personal journey, integrity, or value systems, to allow them to highlight their EQ strength. However, if they are unable to decide, then you can pick something that is directly relevant to the current state of the company or day-to-day needs of the role.

STEP 3: PICK EXPERIENCE TYPE

For most people, reflecting on genuinely meaningful life experiences (positive or negative) allows them to draw on and exhibit the emotional part of that journey. Allowing them to pick an experience—ideally a challenging situation they overcame or a meaningful milestone they are proud of—that shaped them, personally or professionally, and one they are comfortable sharing will allow you, as the interviewer, to get deeper insights into their emotional intelligence.

STEP 4: FRAME THE QUESTION

Now it's time for you to clearly frame your question. You have the choice of starting broad at a macro level or to be more detailed and use a micro lens to ask the question.

SCORING EQ

I recommend scoring candidates using a simple and directional scorecard that marks the EQ levels as either *high*, *medium*, or *low*. Most CEOs and hiring managers are time poor and recognize that in the case of EQ, they are ultimately trying to assess directional capabilities of the candidate relative to the needs of the role, as highlighted by the EQ Matrix. Hence staying away from complex tools and scoring methodologies helps avoid false precision without yielding incremental benefits.

Each of the EQ traits are exploratory pathways to help you uncover emotional intelligence in the candidates. Drive explores what motivates the candidates and if they recognize the source and power of their motivations and how their experiences and journeys have shaped them.

Self-awareness, self-development, and honest learnings are all grounded in deeper introspective abilities, helping them identify their distinctive skills, willingness to learn, coachability and ability to coach others, and even willingness to struggle to get to a better end state. Teamwork naturally explores their desire and ability to work with others versus working alone, their principles and practices to influence others around them (juniors, peers, and seniors), and their ability to handle organizational evolution and change. Empathy is all about finding out if the candidate can understand and share feelings with the intention of exploring their ability to handle and communicate during stressful situations while also being aware of how others on their team might be feeling during such times.

continued →

At this stage you may choose to conduct your conversation top-down, asking broad, macro questions where you can ask them to describe a situation or an event that they believe has truly shaped them. Alternatively, you may wish to be more directive or specific around their positive or negative experiences with questions around topics such as: the biggest teaching moments that they may have left off their resume; learnings as a leader of an immensely successful or unsuccessful project; types of lessons learned and their impact on them as a leader and the teams they lead; learnings from their toughest professional experience; identifying their distinctive spike or something they believe is missing from their ideal professional arc.

David Brown, a UK-based mental performance and leadership expert who is mentor to several world champion Formula 1 drivers, European soccer champions, and global executives, put it this way:

> It's hard to inspire when you're not inspired, and it's hard to lead others if you're not leading yourself. EQ is the foundation to mastery of these fundamentals.[3]

AN EQ SELF-REFLECTION EXERCISE

For interviewers, doing a self-reflective exercise to understand their own EQ levels can be insightful, fun, and beneficial. As part of leadership capability development in an organization, I ask CEOs and their teams a simple question: What are your own EQ levels?

You can use the above EQ Deep Dive Framework to see how you would answer the questions as if you were being interviewed by someone. What examples would you share, and how would you score yourself on the high-medium-low scale? This is a great exercise to help you increase self-awareness and work with those around you. It will also help you prepare for interviewing for EQ by allowing you to better appreciate and empathize with candidates as they try to navigate this topic in a high-pressure interview situation.

Next, identify *who* will be in the interview. Based on the role and the way your process is organized, you'll want to include other executives, board members, senior management, and possibly peers. As a CEO or an investor interviewing C-level executives, you will want to get an opinion from at least one or two other executives (usually at the board level) in the company. If you are hiring functional leaders, it might be important to have functional or department heads involved in the process. For example, if you are hiring a Controller or SVP of IT, you will want to have the CFO, COO, and a couple of key business unit heads involved.

Getting the candidates to be interviewed by their future direct reports is slightly tricky. Some people believe that direct reports should interview their future boss. I disagree; however, at some stage—ideally when the likely winning candidate is closer to the finish line—facilitating such conversations can be invaluable. I tend to avoid an official interview with direct reports for several reasons. First, there are several occasions when the search for a new leader is a confidential process where the incumbent leader (to be replaced) and their team is unaware of upcoming changes. If you are doing an external search, it also suggests that you may have already determined that no internal candidate was qualified to step up into the role. In both these instances, it becomes counterproductive to have the incumbent team be involved in the process. If, on the other hand, the process is not confidential, the future leader being evaluated by the same people they will have to evaluate in the job can feel lopsided; such interviews can lead to unhelpful tension in the system before the team has even started working together.

Then there is the issue of limited time that the candidates have to do their own diligence on the company and team. Most candidates, and particularly those interviewing for senior executive roles, want to spend their short window during the interview process to conduct their own diligence on the company. They will inevitably want to speak with other leaders on key company issues such as business model, current challenges, market opportunity, growth issues, functional gaps and needs, and so on so they can get a better and richer sense of the opportunity and build their view on the guiding principles and values of folks who will be their bosses and peers. Parts of these discussions will naturally reveal organizational opportunities potentially involving their future direct reports.

For time-poor senior candidates, who at this stage are still in discovery mode, adding conversations with direct reports at this stage can be difficult and sometimes a deterrent from staying in the process. But having said that, it is healthy for the direct reports to meet and interact with their potential boss at some stage in the process—just not as an interview. A natural point for it to happen is toward the end of the TAF, during the Close stage and typically after the verbal offer has been accepted—ideally, after the documents have been signed. It can be positioned as a meet and greet in a casual environment such as a group lunch or dinner. Such an interaction allows the junior members to be part of the process, which is a valuable way to achieve successful transitions and increases buy-in. It is also a great professional development practice for those direct reports because, one day, those team members will become managers and will need to interview folks. This informal conversation can be a good foundational experience where there is no interview and therefore no associated pressure, but it gives them a lens into such interactions. It can reduce (not eliminate) the possibility of them fearing for their jobs when the new boss shows up, and preemptively helps minimize anxiety about what their future boss is like. Both these benefits also help increase employee retention during senior management transitions. The incoming executive or manager will also naturally want to meet the team to add to their diligence on the team and company to develop a sense of the organization they are going to be adopting.

Next, define your perspective on the *how*. This goes back to knowing the process and how you wish to proceed in these next couple of rounds. Does it make sense to have just one intermediate round (before the final case round), or is the position (e.g., faces many stakeholders in the company) and organization structure (multiple business units, international locations, etc.) such that multiple rounds will be necessary? You could have all candidates go in sequence with each of the interviewers or choose to have these conversations in parallel—the latter will improve your process times and help you get to the final slate quicker. Sometimes, to increase process efficiency and reduce the total number of interviews in the process, you can do two-on-one interviews. The key to defining *how* is to find the balance between having your major stakeholders involved in the process versus having fatigued the candidates. In today's highly competitive talent war, time is not your friend. And when compounded with a higher volume of interactions, there is a decent possibility that some candidates (who may also be interviewing in other places) may simply reach their limit and withdraw from the process.

Finally, calibrate to finalize the slate. This is starting to get very exciting. You are now at that stage where your hiring team ideally likes two or three people but needs to align on who makes it on the final slate for the case interviews. The best way to do this is to have a calibration call. The most efficient way to do this call is by having each interviewer go through their rankings live, and you can compare those rankings. If you have a unanimous top three, then you don't need a lengthy discussion other than if those who did not make it to the top three should also be considered for the final case or as good backup candidates should the top three have disappointing case interviews. However, it is likely that there is disagreement or misalignment among the interviewers, in which case, just like with any other business problem, you will have to facilitate a problem-solving session to get to the final slate.

KEY TAKEAWAYS

✓ Use the follow-up rounds to build a story about the candidate by collating and processing data from all interviews and interviewers. Ensure you dedicate time and a process step to calibrating the various interviewers' opinions to create a singular story for each candidate.

✓ While EQ data should be captured throughout the process, dedicate at least twenty minutes of one of the follow-up interviews to evaluate candidates' EQ levels relative to the needs of the company and role.

✓ Depending on the role, identify who is going to participate in the follow-up rounds.

✓ Junior members should not interview their future boss but, where possible, should meet with them informally ideally once an offer has been accepted.

✓ Time is not your friend—be decisive and clinical about who gets onto the final slate that is going to move into the case round.

CHAPTER 12

CASE INTERVIEWS

YOU HAVE DONE THE RESUME REVIEW, spoken to loads of candidates, had your colleagues or board members speak with a few of them, and now you are down to the final two or three. By now, there have been lots of conversations, perhaps some healthy debate between your team on who is the best candidate, and now, all the finalists can potentially do the job. But how do you pick the winner?

Conventionally, after a couple of interviews, managers have relied on verbal data from conversational discussions, combined with their gut feelings about a candidate, to select their favorite and offer the job. It generally happens based on who they got along with most. That could reflect the candidate's approach and personality or interests shared with the interviewer, or derived comfort from having the same background or having gone to the same college or school. This candidate may have had better stories to tell—about work or outside of work—that made them an exciting person to speak with. They may have had the shiniest resume, with the top brands, the loftiest titles, or the most awards. The good news is that all of these factors are extremely important and not necessarily a bad way of figuring out if you have your future employee in front of you. It's not a surprise that hiring with the conventional gut has worked for many in the past. The challenge, though, is twofold.

First, if you are just relying on several people's gut, then how do you select the winner? Does or should the boss always win? That is, are they the only one with decision rights? What if your colleagues and you feel equally excited about two different people? Should the tie breaker be standardized scores, such as SATs or GMATs? Should you decide based on references for each of the final candidates? Should it come down to who is willing to take compensation that is in your budget?

Second, a gut-based perspective can be highly influenced by the mood of the interviewers, the decision-makers, and the candidate. This means that it is possible that, on a different day, the emotional state of the interviewer or decision-maker can potentially lead to a different choice. The goal is to find ways to reduce such variability, so that you're making the *right* decision and not just the one that feels right at this moment. Also, there are occasions when the decision-maker may not have all the technical skills to evaluate the candidate, and additional data-based insights can help bridge the gap. For example, I don't know how to build IT infrastructure or what it takes to manage software developers. Therefore, when trying to hire a CTO, while I can use my instincts for cultural fit and leadership attributes, I need more than my gut to be able to assess strategic, operational, and technical skills.

This is where a case discussion becomes incredibly valuable. The case is a sample project, which only the final slate of candidates complete. They present their solution to a real-life business problem they are likely to face in the role they are applying for. This one exercise adds transformative rigor to your diligence and provides incredibly rich and complementary data points in the form of structured thought pieces, analysis, and insights to evaluate the candidate's knowledge of subject matter, analytic and communication skills, and ability to handle pressure. These additional data points are instrumental in differentiating between the top candidates and are then combined with the hiring team's experience-based judgment and instincts.

I obviously did not invent the concept of the case and its use. It is an old concept thoroughly leveraged in business schools, management consulting, and investment banking. However, I found that it is highly underrated and underused in the operating world, where we are all trying to make similar talent acquisition decisions but with limited talent pool, capability, and capacity.

Karoon Monfared, CEO of private-equity-backed BusPatrol, USA, agrees that case discussions are hugely beneficial:

Interviews are a strange set of discussions where it is so tricky to figure out if someone is just very good at marketing or if they are genuinely good at the job. That's why I use—and I learned this at McKinsey—a case study, as it allows me and my team to test technical and nontechnical skills at the same time. I love participating in these. Also, it sometimes sparks new ideas for my team.[1]

The case should represent a true scenario your business is facing (or is likely to face) and one that the candidate might also be exposed to in the role they are applying for. It should be fact based, such that it uses actual data—such as financials, sales info, organizational info—rather than fictitious information. For a good case discussion and unlike a math problem, there is no one right answer;

just like in the real world, most business problems can have multiple solutions. To be able to extract meaningful and comparative data points across all the candidates, you and your team need to be clear and aligned on what business traits you are solving for by doing the case evaluation.

There are multiple traits that you can examine through a case exercise that add to your instinct or gut feeling:

- Problem-solving skills
- Analytic skills
- Technical skills
- Strategic skills
- Communication skills
- Attention to detail
- Process skills
- Commitment
- Emotional intelligence

The case can be used to find out if the candidate can take the problem that you have given them and present a consistent set of solutions that make business and operational sense and can be implemented. Since there can be multiple ways to solve problems, the idea is to not compare the result to a singular answer that you may have developed but to assess the candidate's ability and approach to get to the answer. Also, this allows you to assess the candidate's depth of experience and the richness of their tool kit to solve such problems. It will help you identify those who have a tool kit and those looking to learn on the job, who need to build a new one from scratch.

With a well-organized case, you get to test the candidate's ability to take the data—what you shared with them, combined with their own experience and market research—analyze it using their problem-solving tool kit, and present useful and actionable insights. This will help you segment the candidates based on their capabilities, which could range from not being able to do much with the data to being able to present insights (the "so what") and actionable strategies. You can use this opportunity to find candidates who can go beyond information and into insights.

Depending on the job at hand, there are some key technical skills that cannot be tested without such a process step. For example, if you are hiring a CFO, testing their ability to put together the three financial statements or a forecasting model is going to be an important technical skill to assess. Or if you are hiring a salesperson, their ability to share a process map, business development plan, and sales management tracking tools for your business is going to be key. For a CTO, your case design should test their ability to lead infrastructure projects, manage developers (in-house or third party), develop detailed project plans and budgets, and present project milestones with accuracy and completeness.

Going back to the point about insights over information, in most jobs, particularly senior roles, the candidate who has a higher chance of succeeding in a case discussion is the one who can truly combine their experience and strategic muscle with their functional prowess. For example, a sales manager who can show me that they can prioritize certain markets or segments for growth, identify needs of the market, and then use tools such as CRM and trackers to help their team deliver is always going to outshine someone who has done the job for years but will rely on me or others to identify opportunities and define strategic choices for them every step of the way.

Agnostic of the seniority of hire, if a candidate cannot communicate their analysis, insights, views, and questions in a simple, concise, and clear way, they are not going to be a strong employee for you. The case forces candidates to communicate both in writing and verbally. This allows you to differentiate between someone who is a good talker and someone who says something useful and delivers it thoughtfully. Unless it is necessary for the role, allowing your candidates to use their preferred tool (Word, Excel, PowerPoint, etc.) to deliver their solution avoids unnecessary technology hurdles and ensures focus on the content.

Attention to detail is often underestimated as a key to success in most jobs. Most of us will likely not hire someone for the job of a rocket scientist, but, whether your company is a start-up or a profit-breathing giant, an employee with attention to detail can save the day. Some roles (such as production, finance, accounting, engineering, operations) will need a lot more of it than other roles (such as sales, marketing, HR). But they all need it. While behavioral tools can directionally indicate such traits, the case discussion makes the presence and extent of someone's attention to detail clear as day.

Following a process is another must-have in the majority of roles. In many senior positions, a key deliverable is to add or change processes. The absence or presence of such a trait becomes obvious when the person interviewing for the job fails to follow the process outlined for the delivery and presentation of the case. This shows up in contexts such as (but not limited to) not answering the questions in the case, not sending preread materials (proactively or as requested) the day before their presentation, not being ready with the presentation at the time of the call, or not being able to figure out how to use technology to share their documents live. Poor process adherence during a key interview stage can be a good indicator of weak on-the-job process creation or compliance skills.

Whether the candidate's commitment is to the opportunity (do they really want the job, and will they stick through the interview process?) or to the company (will they show up to work and stay with the company?), most employers want to find out there is some commitment before investing more time in a candidate, especially if they are excited about some of the candidates. Most candidates are likely juggling the demands of their current job, and some may also have family commitments. Additionally, if they are being pursued by other companies, the demands on their time are enormous. And since completing the case (analysis, content development, formatting, and presentation) can take up to twenty hours for some roles (more for senior roles), their willingness and commitment to complete the case, go through the entire process, and present something that is thoughtful and respectable requires a level of commitment that is usually a strong indicator of their interest in the job and their commitment to getting things done, as well as a proxy for how they will pursue projects in your organization.

As a case interview is meant to mimic, as closely as practically possible, a true problem-solving and business discussion, it is the best opportunity for you to experience how the candidate will engage, respond, and behave on the job during team and client discussions. Therefore, it presents a great opportunity for you and your team to pay attention to the candidate's levels of emotional intelligence and perhaps dive deeper into any questionable areas discovered during the EQ Deep Dive in previous interview rounds. Table 12.1 presents some points to observe to assess a candidate's EQ during a case discussion.

Table 12.1. Case study observations to assess a candidate's EQ levels

Context	EQ attribute or trait	Observations and data points on EQ levels
Presentation style	1. Respect 2. Listening skills 3. Friendly versus aggressive	How a candidate presents and defends their case can reveal a lot about their EQ levels. 1. Body language—whether it is aggressive or friendly 2. Ability to listen and engage with interview panel in a constructive way versus being defensive/angry
Content	1. Awareness 2. Handling pressure/conflict	Choice of words used to articulate points of view can be very revealing during the case. 1. Exclusive or overwhelming use of the word "I" versus intention of involving/leveraging team can show lack of awareness and overvaluation of self-worth, hence low EQ. 2. Questions around cultural and behavioral impact will also reveal levels of awareness and ability to think about soft topics as they relate to the impact of the role (and its responsibilities). 3. Handling disagreements with ease versus in a confrontational manner

Content and Process

The content and process of the case interview can be a game changer in separating the bad, the good, and the best to get to the winner. It is your job to make sure that the structure and content of the materials you share with the candidates are fit for purpose.

Start by keeping it real. Using real and fact-based information in the case is key to a nonhypothetical strategic and thoughtful conversation. Don't make up your data. It not only defeats the purpose of finding out what the candidate would do in real life but also makes it harder for you to assess the viability of their solutions. Just imagine trying to make up the company's financials or operational data such that they make sense while being fake. It is hard enough as it is to go through this process; don't make it extra hard for yourself. Make the candidates sign NDAs, and use real numbers and scenarios.

Amit Shah, COO of Virta Health, USA, shared how he uses this approach:

> For select candidates, I always give them a mini-project. It's usually a problem my team is working on. In fact, my team comes up with the project to give to candidates. It's not only a great way to find analytic and communication skills but [also] a chance for the candidate to learn a bit about our company and a real problem we are facing.[2]

Include quantitative aspects. Whether you are looking for a C-level executive or a mid-level employee, they are all going to need (and hopefully want) to process quantitative information associated with their roles. In today's businesses, while the scope of the role increases as folks move up the organizational hierarchy, every employee's work can be attributed to a quantitative outcome that feeds an overall change in enterprise value of the business. Their ability to manage, process, and analyze the data is the only way for you to know their true quantitative muscle.

However, don't just focus on quant. As a quant jock, in my early days of hiring people on my teams, I was often exclusively focused on the quantitative aspects, as they were easier for me to test. However, in my latter years I realized that it is not just about the numbers. Equally important is for candidates to think through process implications, organizational tweaks, influencing techniques, and technological enablement ideas to effect systematic and scalable change as part of their proposal. Including questions around the *how* and *who* as it relates to implementation of their ideas will allow you to test the validity of their quantitative solutions.

Ensure you only ask focused and relevant questions in the case study. It is very easy to throw the kitchen sink into these exercises with the hope that candidates will give you something to chew on. That is a terrible strategy, because not only will that confuse the candidates, but it will also make them do heaps more work that may not be very exciting or palatable for them. Also, the more you ask them to do, the more you will need to review, which means you will need more time and energy. For the sake of efficiency while staying true to the purpose of the case for the role being filled, it is important to be clinical with your questions and in alignment with what you are solving for. If I give a CFO candidate questions about sales and marketing, technology, or Lean Six Sigma—none of which they will have any control over— then not only have I wasted their time, but I also did not learn how good they are at running the finance function. Role-specific content is the best way to identify the ideal person for the job.

CASE STUDY EXAMPLE: EXECUTIVE

CHARACTERISTICS TO ASSESS (FOR HIRING TEAM USE ONLY)

- *Strategic thinking and market or industry knowledge:* the candidate's ability to set growth vision, keeping in mind macro and micro trends both outside and inside the business

- *Planning and prioritization:* their ability to design and prioritize short- versus long-term initiatives and must-have versus nice-to-have projects

- *Financial knowledge:* their ability to understand, analyze, derive, and track actionable financial insights that can inform strategy and measure financial impact

- *Organizational design:* people practices (acquisition, performance, retention, development), organizational design experience, and cultural implications of change

- *Analytic and synthesis skills:* quantitative and qualitative analytic ability to go beyond information into actionable insights to develop and implement growth strategies

- *Communication skills:* their ability to succinctly present and manage pressure or confrontation when challenged

QUESTIONS FOR DISCUSSION (SHARED WITH CANDIDATES)

Overall

- *Industry and market trends:* Please discuss your understanding and the implications of macro and market (current and future) trends of our industry.

- *Strategy and initiatives:* Based on the above, please share a prioritized set of strategic initiatives that you would pursue to improve the long-term enterprise value of our business.

- *Technology or digital:* Please share the technology or digital trends you see in the market, and highlight opportunities for our business to leverage or manage those trends.

continued →

Company-Specific Insights

- *Financials:* (1) Please use the financial data provided to share your views and implications of key financial trends in the business. (2) Based on your recommended strategies and needs of the business, what financial KPIs would you prioritize monitoring for this business, and why?

- *People:* (1) Please share your high-level observations on the company's organizational structure shared with you. (2) Are there any key roles or responsibilities that you believe should be added into the structure? Please explain why. (3) How would you prioritize any suggested organizational changes?

Product and Pricing Trends

- Using the data shared, are there any product or pricing trends that you observe at the company, division, or customer level?

- How do these trends compare to the market and how does that influence your growth strategy for our business?

CASE STUDY EXAMPLE: SALES MANAGER

CHARACTERISTICS TO ASSESS (FOR HIRING TEAM USE ONLY)

- *Functional expertise:* business development, sales management, sales delivery and tracking, CRM and data analytics, and customer life cycle management

- *Planning and prioritization:* time management, pipeline management, proposal prioritization

- *Market knowledge:* knowledge of customer needs, familiarity with competitive landscape, pricing insights

- *People leadership:* people practices (team building, performance management, development) and ability to work with cross-functional teams (ops, IT, systems, admin, etc.)

- *Communication skills:* ability to develop and present sales pro-posals and handle pressure/confrontation when challenged

QUESTIONS FOR DISCUSSION (SHARED WITH CANDIDATES)

Overall

- *Industry and market trends:* Please discuss your understanding and the implications of macro and our industry-specific market (current and future) trends.

- *Competitive landscape:* Share your views on our current competitive landscape, our distinctive advantages and areas of improvement, and any recommendations for change.

- *Technology/digital:* Please share the technology/digital trends you see in the market, and highlight opportunities for our business to leverage/manage those trends.

Company-Specific Insights

- *Sales:* (1) Based on the data shared with you, what are your insights on the company's business development and sales efforts, and do you have any recommendations for change? (2) Share your proposal to double our sales in the next three years. Please include specific short- and long-term initiatives you would like to pursue. (3) Provide details of your work plan (timelines and deliverables) to meet the above goal. (4) Identify tools and resources you will need to execute your plan.

- *People:* (1) Please share your high-level observations on the company's sales organizational structure. (2) Are there any key roles or responsibilities that you believe should be added into the structure? Please explain how you would prioritize those changes. (3) What tools and processes do you use to manage performance and develop your sales teams?

Product and Pricing Trends

- Are there any product or pricing trends that you observe at the company, division, or customer level?

- How do these trends compare to the market, and how does that influence your growth strategy for our business?

CASE STUDY EXAMPLE: OFFICE ADMINISTRATOR

CHARACTERISTICS TO ASSESS (FOR HIRING TEAM USE ONLY)

- *Tactical knowledge:* ability to schedule meetings, complete billing (AR and AP), generate reports, and be familiar with various software (billing, timekeeping, Microsoft office, etc.)

- *Specific traits:* some of these typically include having high attention to detail, written and verbal communication skills, ability to take coaching/feedback, and high sense of urgency

QUESTIONS FOR DISCUSSION (SHARED WITH CANDIDATES)

Tactical Knowledge

- *Scheduling:* (1) Share (in writing) the details of your process to schedule meetings, especially when many internal and external parties are involved. (2) What principles do you use to prioritize scheduling some meetings over others?

- *Billing:* (1) Provide (in writing) a detailed overview of your billing process and timeline. (2) What billing software are you familiar with? (3) What reports do you run/review daily/weekly/monthly when it comes to billing?

- *The use of tools:* (1) What are your favorite tools for all aspects of your work? (2) What tools do you wish you had to be even more efficient, and why?

Additional/Alternative Short Deliverables

- Can you share (in writing) your view of a day and a week in your life in this role?

- What are some of your insights based on a review of the report we shared with you? (*You can share AR, AP, timekeeping, or any other report relevant to what you plan on having this role review or produce.*)

- What are some of your insights based on a review of the email we shared with you? (*You can share a sample email to an employee, vendor, or customer to see if the candidate can spot any errors—punctuation, grammar, numerical data, and so on—to test their ability to be detail oriented.*)

A well-organized process is going to help you stay efficient and reveal useful comparable traits about your candidates. Make sure you have each of the candidates sign an NDA before sharing any confidential company materials. This is the buy-in for the candidate to ensure they are open to receiving the content and maintaining confidentiality. Once the NDA is signed, it is good practice to send a detailed email (see below) that includes the company-level data, outlines what and when things are expected from them, indicates a point of contact for scheduling, and lists the members of the case interview panel and key milestones. This level of detail and clarity is critical for the candidates to plan and for you to ensure successful execution of this step of the Talent Acquisition Funnel.

Since some of the candidates may have current jobs and personal commitments, it is thoughtful and kind to include a weekend in the preparation time. You should allow a level playing field by giving all of them the same amount of time to review and prepare the materials. It is also helpful to offer each candidate the option of an additional call with you or other members of the hiring team to answer any questions on the company-level detailed content they received from you. This is voluntary on their part, giving them an opportunity, if they deem it necessary, to best understand the materials and any new questions that come up. Whether a candidate takes you up on this offer should not affect your judgment of their candidacy. The content of their presentation and the discussion is what will matter the most at the end of the day.

The case builds a mountain of practical information on top of your gut instincts, giving you the confidence you need to get the best person for the job. This process, at a minimum, sifts out those who are not going to be able to make it in the real job. So just like the

---

CASE INTERVIEW EMAIL SAMPLE TEMPLATE

As discussed on our last call [*assuming this was previously discussed with each candidate*], attached are some supporting confidential materials for your review. This is to help you prepare for next week's [include the date and time, including the time zone, here] strategy (case) discussion with select board members of [company name]. Below are a few associated process points.

DOCUMENTS ATTACHED

- *Case discussion:* outlines the discussion topics or questions we would like you to address during the board discussion

- *Strategy discussion—supporting materials:* additional data on the company you may find helpful, including select data in Excel for your review and analysis

PROCESS

- *Call with me or my team:* We can make ourselves available for a 30-minute call in case you wish to clarify any attached content or process topics. Please reach out to schedule.

- *Presentation to the board:* This will be 60 minutes [include the date and time, including the time zone, here] (calendar invites will be coming from our assistant, who is copied on this email).

- *Participants:* My colleagues (copied), other members of the board, and the CEO of [company name] will be joining the discussion.

- *Presentation materials:* We suggest you use your preferred method and tools to make and share the presentation. To allow for a rich discussion, please send us any preread materials at least 24 hours prior to the meeting.

Please feel free to reach out if you have any questions on the above, and we look forward to the case discussion.

---

leadership and behavioral tools, it prevents you from hiring the wrong person. But most importantly, it shines light on the winner: I have not yet had one situation, whether hiring a CEO or an admin team member, where a case discussion has not helped me identify who stands out and will bring the most to my organizations. What you will find is that the winner is not only able to deliver on well-structured great content (written, verbal, and visual) when answering the required case questions but also able to lead a thoughtful discussion with the interviewing team, leaving people confident about their candidacy and likelihood of success as a future teammate.

KEY TAKEAWAYS

✓ To get the best candidate you can afford, avoid relying exclusively on good chats and gut feelings: Go beyond conversation and into specific outputs.

✓ A case is a tactical avenue to be able to assess the skills of the candidates that are sometimes hard to evaluate with general conversations and resume reviews. A case can reveal key skills including problem-solving, analytics, communication, technical and process capabilities, attention to detail, level of commitment to the process, and enthusiasm for the job.

✓ Use real data, real business scenarios, and questions that the candidate will be tackling in the job.

✓ Ask questions that are relevant to the role. The higher your focus, the more likely you are going to get a true read on their ability to perform on the job.

✓ Use scenarios and questions that cover both quantitative and qualitative outcomes associated with the role.

✓ Clear communication of the steps for candidates to follow maintains the sanctity of your process for them as much as for you.

CLOSE

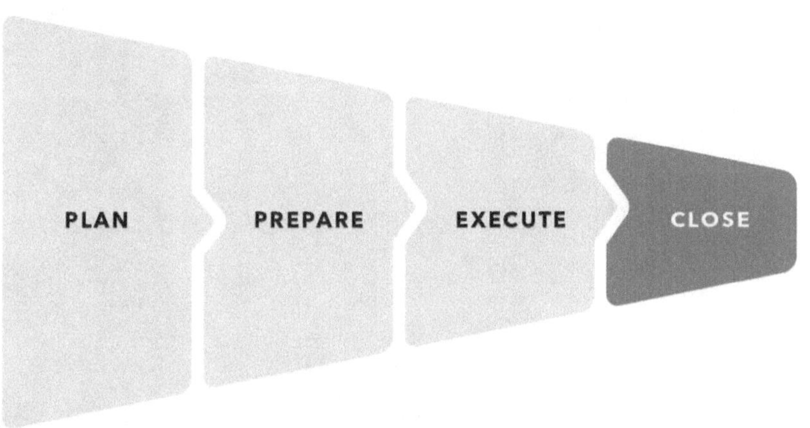

CHAPTER 13

CALIBRATE

GETTING BACK TO THE CANDIDATES QUICKLY, especially if you have found the winner, gives you the capability to compete with others who might also be trying to acquire the same talent. There are a few tactical steps that you should follow as soon as you have completed the case interviews. And this applies even if your interviews are spread across an entire week.

The very first thing you need to do is calibrate the points of view of everyone who was involved in the case interview process. The goal here is to see if there is alignment on the overall decision of who should be turned down and if there is a majority—if not unanimous—lean toward the winner. Just like the initial interview tiers, the three specific buckets to use for categorization are *definite hire*, *backup*, and *definite turndown*. If you have a clear definite hire—the winner—decide (either as a committee or individually) and stick to it. The backup (unless you have loads of potential backups, in which case I am envious) will usually be one other candidate that the hiring team felt was close to winning. You want to keep this person in the mix, especially in the event the winner does not materialize (the candidate turns the offer down for another opportunity, the two parties could not align on terms, their references reveal an issue, or the background check comes back dodgy, etc.); then this person could also be considered for the role. The rest of the group need to be informed of the turndown decision. It is critical that you do this for two reasons. First, it is professional best practice and the right thing to do to let people know where they are in the process. Second, I have seen some companies who like to "hang on" to candidates simply because they don't have conviction in their own decision-making. Just because you cannot get your stuff together does not mean that you keep other professionals hanging.

At this stage of the Talent Acquisition Funnel, it probably has been at least six to eight weeks since you internally discussed some of the specifics about the role. Also, it is possible that, in the same time frame, the specific needs of the company may have evolved slightly. Therefore, it is a great opportunity to align on a few critical items relative to the job description to align on purpose and vision for the role. What are the key items this role must deliver to be successful in the position? What are the EQ levels needed for this role? Is the title remaining the same? The title discussion is particularly important if there is going to be a major shift in the company's position at this late stage in the game, unless you are open to giving a more senior title (for example, from VP of Finance to CFO or from Head of Operations to COO) to a candidate. Any title downgrade without clear discussion and consultation with the winner will shock the winner and could result in them exiting the process. The next set of conversations with the winner is going to revolve around compensation, so you should confirm the annual base salary, the target annual bonus, and any equity or long-term incentives (and at what valuation) that will constitute the final offer.

It is also important to decide on clear next steps for each of the items mentioned above. Specifically, as a hiring team you need to align on the following:

- Who is going to make the call to the winner?
- When is that call going to be made?
- What is that person going to share on the call?

In the event there is a recruiting partner, determine who is going to communicate to them about the decision. For those in the potential backup and turndown buckets, does it make sense for someone from your team to call each person, or do you prefer that message be delivered by the recruiting partner (assuming you are using one)? Keeping the recruiting firm closely in the loop on this part of the process not only makes the close effective but also helps you avoid crossed wires and the market's perception that the company is uncoordinated, which occasionally can end up costing you the winning candidate.

Finally, execute. Speed wins! One of the most powerful things that I observed at Wharton was that, regardless of the organization that was on campus recruiting MBAs—McKinsey, Goldman Sachs, Google, a private equity firm—none of them wasted any time between making their decisions and calling the winning candidates to congratulate them. Sometimes it was the same day, and worst case it was the next day. In the operating world, where you don't have an army of people to make all this happen, I strongly suggest that you at least make the following happen to gain some of that competitive advantage you are seeking:

- You as the CEO or the hiring manager should prioritize calling the winner personally within twenty-four hours of making the decision. The sooner you can move on this, the higher the likelihood that you will get the candidate to sign up.

- Let others in the backup and definite turndown buckets know within forty-eight hours, and leverage your recruiting partners in this part of the process. Don't be a hero; use the team you have around you to help.

Samantha Foster, Managing Director and leader of the Global Industrials Practice at talent advisory firm ZRG Partners, USA, spoke of the problems with taking too much time to nail down a first-choice candidate:

> When a company moves at a slow pace, it is usually because they haven't made candidates the priority and cleared space on their calendars. This leaves the candidates feeling underwhelmed by the company's commitment to the role. Additionally, slow decision-making opens the opportunity for a candidate to collect competing offers. Companies need to be committed, be decisive, and generate a compelling offer to the candidate.[1]

People have often asked me how much or how little to share on these calls after the case interview. I say that, ultimately, you want to make sure that your preferred candidate accepts the offer and every other candidate is treated respectfully and leaves having a positive, professional view of you and your company. Don't stress that those who did not get the job don't like you; instead, make sure you don't give them any obvious reasons for speaking disparagingly about you in the market. Some specific questions to have thought through before you make these calls will not only help close on the candidate; they will also allow your team to accelerate the back-end process of pulling together a formal offer and preparing for the next steps in the TAF.

- Are you planning to simply congratulate the winner, or do you plan to also share specifics of some or all elements of the offer including compensation, titles, benefits, and so on?

- When will the first congratulatory call be made, and will the caller, talent acquisition champion, or the lead recruiter also try to get soft verbal alignment on terms (compensation, title, and start date) of the offer?

- Will you be communicating any contingencies, such as completion of reference and background checks associated with the offer?

- When will there be a written offer, and will that be more along the lines of an offer letter or a legal contract?

KEY TAKEAWAYS

✓ Just like at the end of the follow-up interview rounds, calibrate with the panel that was part of the case interview to identify the winner.

✓ Move quickly after the case rounds to decide on the winner, when the panelists' memories are fresh and more importantly to increase your chances of getting a verbal commitment from the candidate.

✓ Revisit the fundamentals for the position, title, compensation, and key success metrics to be able to communicate clearly and precisely with the winner.

✓ Take no more than twenty-four hours after the case rounds are completed to let the winner know that they will be receiving an offer. The longer you wait, the greater the chance that you could lose the candidate.

CHAPTER 14

COMMIT

MAKING AN OFFER TO A CANDIDATE is one of the most exciting things I have been lucky enough to do many times in my life. While it is a lot of work for both the company and the winning candidate to get to this point, it is extremely gratifying to be able to share such great news. Not to mention, it brings the excitement of being able to fill the role and grow your business. While anyone can pick up the phone and give good news, and most people like giving good news, what we have to remember is that the deal has not closed yet and there is still some selling to do. There is an art to making this call, and it can differentiate you from the rest of your competition.

For a start, the commitment call is an opportunity to demonstrate your company's excitement to the winner. You must remember that there are two buyers in this game, and now the stake for you is potentially slightly higher than for the candidate, particularly in competitive situations in which the candidate may have other offers they are entertaining, including the possibility of their current employer wanting to retain them. So, while it's an exciting moment, you can't quite start celebrating victory yet. It's like in sports, where you are down to the last two minutes and up by a few points but are up against a passionate and equally driven counterparty—in this case all other employers competing for the same talent. You would agree that now would not be the time to let up. Making an offer requires a few simple yet often neglected or underestimated execution steps.

First, *don't outsource this call.* Do it yourself! Whether you run the company, division, function, or team, this is the time to own it and take the ball across the finish line. Outsourcing the call to the recruiting partners or someone else on your team is not only unnecessary but, candidly, won't deliver the same passion and oomph that you have for this person and the role.

Show your excitement! Start with the big bang of congratulations and what it would mean to have the winner join your team. It sounds obvious, but you will be shocked how many managers, CEOs, investors, and others forget to congratulate the winner and get right into specifics of the offer, sharing feedback and a bottom-up build-up to the "aha" moment. When you deliver the message, do it emphatically. If you and the recipient don't get goose bumps or, at a minimum, a jump in your heart rates, then what's the point? Your energy and enthusiasm will have a tremendous positive impact on the candidate and will increase your ability to close on them.

Remember, it's a big moment for them. This is a massive moment for most (if not all) employees. If you just hired a C-level candidate, that does not happen often in most people's lives. And even if it's a junior role, then it is still a momentous occasion for that person as they advance their career, especially if they are now getting a higher title and more money. For them, it is often a game changer. And you get to deliver this news to them. If you sense they don't see it that way, highlight it to them, as sometimes we all need to hear it to believe it.

Retention starts now. While there are a few more things to formally complete before the candidate is officially an employee, your mindset and behaviors should start transitioning into retention mode. In other words, you must think about how to keep the winner engaged and excited. You do that by honestly and sincerely thinking of things you can do to make their experience not just a positive one but an extraordinary one. This includes their offer acceptance experience, the crossboarding experience, and their ability to experience your true coaching and mentoring intent. The other by-product of this mindset is the applicant's excitement for working with someone like you will go up—giving you a competitive edge over competitors who may just view this last bit as a transaction.

Adam Cooper, CEO of Oasis Dates, USA, offered advice for this point in the process:

This is my favorite part—when it all comes together. There should be no surprises if the preclosing has been done along the way. But it's still important to reinforce the unique selling proposition of the opportunity, the company, and the hiring manager all the way through official signing. Don't assume that just because you make an offer, they will accept it; be specific and ask them to confirm they will accept it.[1]

Share specifics. Outline the key terms of the offer. Within microseconds of learning that they have been selected for the job, all they want to hear are the numbers. Everything else you will have said between those two things probably won't register. Some specifics that you will need to share include the following:

- Total cash compensation
- Annual base salary and the pay cycle timing
- Annual target bonus dollars and timing
- Any equity or long-term incentives that you are offering

Make the offer contingent. Since the reference calls and background checks are still to be completed, make sure that the candidate knows that any offer, verbal or written, will be contingent on successful and satisfactory completion of those two steps. This serves two purposes. First, it sets the expectations correctly that the process is not entirely over. This is important, especially for those who have current jobs. It is only fair to them to be fully informed to make their decision on when they can resign from their job or withdraw from other processes. Second, it allows them to preemptively bring up any issues that might surface during the reference calls or background checks that may throw a wrench in the works. This is helpful to you as a hiring manager if you need to recalibrate on the offer before you continue doing even more work pulling offer documents together and scheduling reference calls.

Next, outline what you will be requiring from them. Start with an alignment of terms: I used to waste a lot of time and energy getting the offer documents (offer letters, employment agreements, grant agreements) ready without having had a full alignment on the principal terms of the deal. The goal is not to come to an agreement right then but to let them know that, unless you two do not at least verbally align on the principal terms, it will not be possible for you to share anything in writing. This is essentially like a "soft close," where you and the candidate are aligning—verbally or in writing—on specific terms for the close. Knowing how far apart you are is helpful in trying to figure out if a bridge can be built quickly or if the two parties have drifted too far afield from each other's expectations on the terms of employment. One additional benefit of not putting an offer in writing right away is to avoid them taking the written offer to the next bidder (their current job or another company) and using it to trade up, rather than honestly be engaged with you on the position you are offering. Sadly, this is not a hypothetical situation but one that I have seen candidates do, from C-level roles to GMs and middle managers.

They should now provide you with a list of four to six professional references and will need to complete a form for a background check. You will need the winning candidate to indicate an approximate start date. This is helpful for a few reasons. It indicates commitment—and that they have thought through the timing of exit from their current job. It is an indirect tool to pressure-test if they have true intentions of joining or if they are using your offer as leverage to negotiate other deals. Operationally, it is important to start putting things in motion in your company. This could mean thinking about internal team communications, crossboarding logistics, and formulating a plan for adjusting the team and anyone currently occupying the job. It can also mean triggering logistical items such as ordering hardware, establishing office space, and so on. Finally, for many senior executive searches, this is the time for informing the direct reports, to ensure their retention and cultural sensitivity. Also, for those who will be receiving any form of equity incentive (or similar) that has a vesting schedule, you need to have a start date for when vesting begins. The sooner the better for the employee. This can also serve as an incentive for them to help you complete the reference and background checks quickly as well as formally agree to principal terms of employment.

Next, you'll outline what they should expect from you. This starts with the written offer letter. After you have verbally aligned on the principal terms of the offer, you need to move quickly to get everything in writing. Hand it over to the candidates as a formal offer. For more senior executives, this may mean a formal and legal employment agreement that constitutes other terms such as noncompete, no solicitations, and severance. For more junior roles, you may only end up sending an offer letter. Either way, it is important that you get something in writing to the candidates within forty-eight hours of a verbal agreement. Once again, speed is your friend here. First, it's the right thing to do. Moving quickly means you are more organized, and that is an attractive trait from the point of view of the candidates. It also helps you avoid the candidate changing their mind or the excitement of it all going a bit stale. While it is not wrong to have them express their wish list, there is a limit to the number of iterations you will want to go through. Moving quickly can get to this wish list sooner. Moving quickly also lets you release other candidates who may still be making their way through the earlier steps of the funnel.

The offeree should expect progress updates: Let them know you will try to keep them updated on how the reference calls are going, as well as the likely completion date for the background check (which is often outsourced to other companies). Please note that you are not required to (nor should you) provide a summary of your confidential conversations with the referees. This is purely a process update on reference calls, particularly if you are having any difficulty reaching a referee.

While the final steps are underway, either you may want the candidate to have informal conversations with other team members or the candidates may want the same. This is an entirely optional exercise and depends a lot on the nature of the role, the level of confidentiality, and your comfort in the candidate interacting with your current team members. If you are hiring a C-level executive, it may make sense for them (after they have signed the agreement) to speak with some select members of the senior team. These are folks who were not involved in the acquisition process but are likely to work with the new hire either as peers or as direct reports. Meeting each other allows for easier cross-boarding between the individuals. If the search was confidential, where you don't wish your current employees to know that a material change is imminent or if you perceive that such interactions could be disruptive in the short run, then you may not want to pursue such introductions.

Most employees wish to see the benefits packages available to them as part of the new job, so they should meet with HR or someone overseeing the benefits program in the company. The person who interacts with the candidate will depend on the structure of the company, seniority of the role, and confidentiality of the search.

Finally, while you must still send the docs to the candidate, it is important that you agree on turnaround times to align with the candidate on two specific dates: the date for feedback on content and the drop-dead sign date. If you agree to get them the docs within twenty-four to forty-eight hours, when can they realistically get back to you? It is also important that you agree to a signing date to allow both parties to work toward a unified timeline and to determine necessary intermediate steps.

While many of the above steps may naturally give you reasons to stay connected with the candidate, I encourage you to maintain that connectivity despite the process steps. Remember, you should already be transitioning to retention mode. The last thing you want at this stage of the game is to have to restart the recruiting engines.

KEY TAKEAWAYS

- ✓ Don't outsource the most exciting part of the process; call the winning candidate yourself.

- ✓ Don't forget to congratulate them.

- ✓ Ensure you share the specifics that matter to most candidates: the compensation, title, and any other major items relevant to the job.

- ✓ Align on the content and timelines of what you both will be sharing with each other to get to the finish line.

CHAPTER 15

COMPLETE YOUR DILIGENCE

I always make sure to do reference calls for C-level candidates myself. It is too important of a hire to trust others on this topic, and more importantly, I need to know if I can work with this person. I need to learn from their previous employers if our personalities will work together. Would we be able to problem-solve on what is important and how to drive value? Do they treat people the same way as I do? These questions can only be answered by doing reference and diligence calls yourself.

—**JORGE GROSS**, Managing Partner at Trivest Partners, USA[1]

MANY PEOPLE TREAT REFERENCE CALLS as a formality. A small subset of founders and CEOs even consider it to be a total waste of time, and some don't even bother doing them. Their view is that a candidate is never going to present someone who is going to say anything but good things about them, so why bother? If you happen to be in that group, you may want to rethink your opinion. People are the biggest asset class in your company, and they command the highest levels of investment from your P&L, so the acquisition of those assets should also command the highest levels of due diligence. The Talent Acquisition Funnel makes that happen. And part of that mindset and methodology is to view the reference calls as the final bit of due diligence that you will personally lead to ensure that you acquire the best possible asset into your team.

It is like doing due diligence to buy a company; before you cut a big check, you want to ensure there is nothing funny hiding behind the scenes. This is why you ask detailed questions to industry experts and the company's customers to confirm your view of the business. Specifically, you try to find out if the company operates the way its management has been saying it does, provides service to the levels of its customers' satisfaction, and is competitively well positioned in the market. That helps you decide if you should put money behind that company or not.

As one of the core principles of this book, acquiring the most important asset for your company—talented people—is a major investment decision both in the process and eventually in the employee. If you get the hiring decision wrong, not only are you going to lose significant hours of work and thousands of dollars in the search cost, but you also run the risk of damaging the company culture and reputation, losing other employees, and diluting the enterprise value of your business. Reference calls are your last line of defense before you make this major investment. Take it as seriously as buying a company. That level of diligence will only serve you well.

As a start, while it may be generally true that candidates only provide references who are going to speak highly of them, their expectation is not always accurate. On several occasions over the last two decades, I have spoken with references who had quite unflattering things to say about the candidate. On one occasion, the person did not even know who the candidate was but had heard the name in their department. I am not sure, in each of these situations, what the candidates were thinking, but it helped me avoid a major hiring blunder.

The quality of your due diligence depends crucially on you actually doing it. If you don't call a candidate's references and don't ask the referees insightful questions, you miss the chance to uncover any last-minute red flags—or to confirm that you've made the right choice.

So how to approach reference calls? Act as if you are still interviewing the candidate, albeit getting to know the person through the eyes of their previous organizations and managers. You should come at it from two angles: qualitatively and quantitatively.

For starters, it's best to approach these conversations as a continuation of your diligence and discovery rather than trying to poke holes, find faults, and look for "gotcha" data between what the candidate said during the process and what you wish to discover from these references.

The other goal here is to benefit from the growing pains others may have experienced working with and hopefully developing your future teammate. Your hope is to get a more capable professional than who they were a few years ago, but you can only validate this hypothesis by completing this part of your diligence.

Also, by finding out the limitations of the employee, you can determine how to best fill those gaps around them or adjust some elements of their work scope to increase their chances of success. For example, while I have led several IT implementation projects where I have managed CTOs, heads of product development, and engineers, I have never been able to code and develop technology myself. Hence, if someone doing a reference check on me does not pick up this gap in my skill set and expects me to roll up my sleeves and every now and then do some coding, then I can guarantee that both I and the project will fail. Best those who are doing diligence on me find out this fact during reference calls and augment my capability gaps with the right talent on the team.

The bottom line is that from an employer's perspective, the interview process is not over until you have completed the reference calls and have built a comprehensive view on the candidate across necessary professional, technical, and cultural elements.

As for the quantitative side, let's imagine we're recruiting a senior executive. An average recruiting process timeline for a senior hire is nearly four months to find the right person and have them contractually agree to join your leadership team. To get to this stage, based on my experience and that of others I have spoken with, over one hundred hours of your team's time may be required, across all candidates from the start of the search, before you are able to find the winning person and confirm an offer. Assuming that the blended highly conservative hourly rate for you and your colleagues is at $200 (it often is significantly higher), then your team has invested nearly $20K to get to this single candidate for this one role. If you end up using recruiting partners for your channel, to get to this point in the Talent Acquisition Funnel may cost you an additional two-thirds of the first-year cash compensation for this role. That tab usually runs in the hundreds of thousands for a C-level hire. But even for an early- to mid-level manager earning, let's say, $100K annually, you will have likely spent $25K–$30K (assuming 30 percent of annual salary, a typical fee for recruiters) on recruiting fees. In total, you might have spent nearly $45K to find this one candidate.

So, what is my point? Well, it's simple: Mathematically the company has completed fourteen of the eighteen steps of the TAF; that's nearly 80 percent of the way to the finish line. The last 20 percent includes three to four hours (assuming you end up doing six calls for thirty minutes each with some additional admin time) of reference calls. Essentially you need less than 5 percent of the time you have already spent to get to this stage to build a higher level of confidence in your investment decision. Having invested $45K already into the process (and that number is much higher for more expensive hires) why would you not invest an addition 5 percent on reference calls? The ROI on this step, through the lens of risk management and value creation, is irrefutable.

Karoon Monfared, CEO of BusPatrol, USA, told me:

It is surprising to me how many companies don't do reference or background checks to complete diligence. I don't even go to a restaurant without looking at reviews. Why would you give up the chance to speak to a prior employer and find out first-hand about the person you are about to hire or make sure they don't have a criminal record by doing a background check?[2]

Now that we have some sense of what is at stake here, let us jump on to the process and content of the reference calls so you can make the most of this last bit of diligence.

Process

Keep reference calls short—a maximum of thirty minutes per call. The person you are speaking with likely has other commitments on their calendar. Also, after the first couple of calls, you are likely going to have enough information to allow you to probe into a different area of investigation or you may be able to have shorter calls.

Ideally, try to get all the calls scheduled within a few days of each other so you can quickly build on the information and, if needed, ask the candidate to provide additional references or background. And if you run into roadblocks, you can always flex your schedule to offer to speak with the references at odd hours. After all, you need to speak with them more than they need to connect with you.

The categories or types of referees depends on the level you are hiring for. For executive candidates, you should ask for at least four and sometimes six references across three buckets. You will need two bosses, two peers, and two direct reports.

The bosses could be their direct supervisors, board members, or investors. The goal is to learn about the executive's leadership skills, technical capabilities, and general management skills set. However, it is understandable that an executive may not have informed their immediate bosses about their departure. In this case, it is fair to accept supervisors from previous roles and companies.

The peers could be other C-level colleagues who report to the same bosses, other GMs or division leaders on the executive leadership committee, or other functional leaders in the organization. Having referees who sit on the same boards as the candidate is also a good reference channel to explore. Ultimately, you are most interested in how the executive partnered with other functional leaders in the business, how they managed up to their boss, and the perception of the executive across the organization.

The direct reports should have worked with the executive for at least twelve months and, ideally, for a couple of years. Any shorter time frame usually does not give enough visibility into the executive's management style and leadership skills.

For mid-level management roles, you should ask for four references: two supervisors and two direct reports. The supervisors are for the same reasons as above. Direct reports are more critical than peers, as you are likely hiring for a tactical leadership role and it will be good to understand the manager's current approach to leading teams and projects. This bit of diligence is going to give you a much better view into the areas where they will be able to stand alone and places where you will need to coach them.

Much like the offer call, you should make these calls yourself as the CEO. You want to make sure that you have found the winner, so don't outsource it to your assistant, an HR manager, a recruiting partner, or someone junior on the team. Either you care or you don't. Make sure you speak with as many references as practically possible. Of course, if you simply don't have the capacity, then give the task to someone you trust, such as the talent acquisition champion or a level 2 leader in your organization who has previously led such calls. If possible, I highly recommend having one other person join the calls with you. While you should lead the call, having someone else with you can add a bit of variety to your calls. It also allows you to train others in your organization, which allows for scalability.

Finally, if you sense any red flags from any one referee, validate on your other calls and eventually with the offeree. If you hear incredibly unfavorable feedback from a referee or across referees, then that may be enough to rescind the offer. In addition to content, the fact that a candidate may have chosen someone who would say highly unfavorable things speaks to the candidate's poor judgment. Also, you don't have time for social references with someone who played golf, fished, or went to high school with the candidate; the fact that they supplied a nonprofessional reference is also a warning sign. The inherent deep bias in social references makes them very difficult to trust and apply in a business setting. I have been on reference calls where the reference did not have much to say about the candidate. Whether it was their natural personality to not speak much or they did not care for the candidate, at a minimum, it's a nonreference. But it is also a red flag that the candidate chose such a reference. Old references—someone who has not worked with the candidate for more than five years—is another major issue. In certain cases, exceptions such as long tenure in one company could be made, but our goal is to learn about the current skills and attitude of the person we are hiring. A window into their skills from more than five years ago doesn't help you see who they are now.

The last cautionary category is unknowledgeable references. These are people who may have worked in the same company at the same time as the candidate but cannot speak to any of the skills you are investigating. For example, I recently did a reference check for a COO who gave names of people who worked in the same company as her. While they knew who she was and had a good opinion of her as a person, they could not share any specifics about her general management or operational skills, strategic knowledge, or people leadership skills. A lack of direct knowledge of the skill set is once again a nonreference for me and needs to be substituted for a true referee.

Content

This is the fun part, as you get to learn about the person you are most excited to hire, and the key to content is intention. Specifically, our goal is to learn more about our top asset so that our investment (both financial and future capacity used for coaching and mentoring) in them is going to help us and the company achieve the goals we have underwritten with this hire. Also, it is important that you make those intentions abundantly clear to the referee to allow for the right framing and tone of the discussion. This will allow you to get thoughtful partnership from the person you called and land your pointed questions without awkwardness.

Before we launch into the specific categories and questions, there are a few preparatory items to keep in mind prior to these calls. First, identify key focus areas based on the role you are trying to fill. Build on the data you have already collected through the interview process—such as doubts on the candidate's ability to prioritize or a desire to dig deeper into their EQ or leadership style. Select the categories you wish to explore based on the referee's likely experience with the candidate and how long ago they may have worked together. Learn from each reference call and build on them; there is no point asking the same question repeatedly, especially if the feedback is consistent. Perhaps explore a different category or go deeper into a category with each successive referee. Finally, it's okay to cut the conversation short. If the reference is not knowledgeable or is from years ago or you have all the information you need, feel free to end the call. But keep it professional.

Now for the questions. Remember, we're looking for insight, not information. If you ask standard questions, you are likely going to get standard answers. Basic answers will not validate or invalidate your views on the candidate. Similar to the approach during the interview rounds, you can ask thoughtful, data-seeking, alternative questions that can transform your insights on the winning candidate. These questions fall into the categories below.

EMPLOYMENT

A stereotypical question like, *Did the person work for you from Date 1 to Date 2 and in this role?* will give you very little useful insight. The reference call is not a resume chronology check; remember, that will get done separately when you get the formal background check done. You want to ask efficient questions that can both verify a few basic items and give you the diligence data you need. You might ask instead, *Can you please share some context of your working relationship with the candidate?*

Ask about the title and roles and responsibilities of the candidate when the referee last worked with them. This is to confirm information the candidate shared in their resume and to compare notes on their titles and roles and responsibilities they had. Some candidates embellish, and the reference call can illuminate that fact immediately.

STRENGTHS

Ask for a list of strengths. Typically, most hiring managers may ask the referee, *What are the strengths of this person?* But you could more subtly ask, *When you think about this person, what is the one thing that stands out for you?* If someone chosen as a referee—essentially, the spokesperson for the candidate—cannot remember one thing that makes the candidate stand out professionally, then the rest of the call is likely going to be average. This is an immediate yellow flag. Even if it has been a few years or the referee had several direct reports, most referees can remember at least a couple of key things about the candidate. You are just hoping that they will give you more than a couple of bullet points. This way, you can build on what they say or recognize that this may not be a content rich conversation.

Another way to ask is, *What skills did you rely on this person the most for? Or what did their team find most inspiring about the person?* This version gets to the heart of the skill set exhibited by the candidate, and you can map it back to the skills you are looking to fill. This is another way to determine strengths and get to a more tactical outcome.

WEAKNESSES

Everyone has things they should never do. For me, it's IT. I suck at it. Ask the reference, *Is there any task or functional responsibility the candidate should not be given?* A general question on weakness such as, *What are their weaknesses?* may lead to a general answer. By being more specific and trying to get to a single attribute, you are likely going to get a more thoughtful answer that you can actually use when you hire the person. For instance, I have hired CEOs who did not get digital functions as part of their portfolio, CFOs who did not get to oversee HR, and COOs who did not manage the tech team based on this part of my due diligence. Had I not asked the questions this way, I might have given them this portfolio of responsibilities only to find out that I did not set up these executives for success and diluted the impact on the organization.

A more positive way to ask the question is, *Given you are clearly invested in this person's growth and success, what is the one area you wish this person would develop going forward as they progress through the ranks?* This version allows the referee to get away from what happened in the past or a traditional weakness answer but nudges them to really think as a mentor or coach to the candidate, which results in a much more thoughtful conversation.

Or you could try, *Given your close professional relationship with this person, is there an area that they have been trying to develop but have not made much progress and why?* This is a twist to the above question if the referee says that they cannot think of much. What is interesting is that if they struggle to give you an answer to this question as well, then there is a chance that either it has been a while since they worked together or they did not work together that closely. Both of those scenarios lead to an average level of credibility and value of this reference call.

ATTENTION TO DETAIL

Attention to detail is not usually discussed by most hiring managers during reference checks. This is a skill set that is extremely important for most roles but specifically for C-level and technical roles, where executives are individually and collectively leading the rest of the organization through complex changes. Having a good sense of this skill set will give you the ability to determine where you as their boss will have leverage versus where you will need to pay particular attention when they or their teams produce content for the company.

You might ask, *On a scale of 0 to 10, where 10 is the most detail-oriented person you have worked with and 0 is someone who has no attention to detail, where does this person rate?* Folks often struggle with the question when asked at a qualitative level, either because no referee wants to say that the candidate has poor attention to detail, or they simply don't know how to give a relative comparison, or they themselves may not have a high level of attention to detail. Offering a scale often makes it easier for people to give you a directional answer.

Another way to back into poor detail orientation is to ask, *Did you find yourself spotting errors in the work product from this person?*

How big were these errors and how frequently did you spot them? It is important to ask the frequency question, so you are able to normalize the issues you hear before assuming it is a consistent issue with the candidate's performance.

PEOPLE SKILLS

For any leadership role, EQ is no longer an optional trait. If the candidate does not have any form for EQ, they are going to struggle in most businesses. This is one of my top three traits to explore during the reference calls. You will have picked up on the candidate's level of EQ (using the EQ Matrix) during the earlier stages of the TAF, and these questions are a way to corroborate your observations thus far. This is a great opportunity to validate your observations on communication approach, conflict management, leadership consistency, listening skills, coachability and coaching skills, or any other people skills that will either be important to success in the role or where you may still have some doubts about the candidate's EQ levels.

You might start with, *How do you think the candidate's direct reports would describe them as a person and a leader?* A leading indicator of leadership effectiveness is employee retention, so you could ask, *What was the level of voluntary attrition that happened under the candidate's watch?*

To quantify their EQ, you could ask, *On a scale of 0 to 10, where 0 is a robot and 10 is the most emotionally aware professional you can think of, how would you score this person?* Again, the scaling helps those who struggle to provide specifics to give you a directional sense of the EQ of the candidate.

Finally, *What three words would you use to best describe this person's leadership skills?* Limited word options can be a very useful way to help the person prioritize what stands out about the candidate. You are hoping to hear words that speak to high-EQ skills (such as *empathetic, good listener, very collaborative*) and not just IQ topics.

A SENSE OF URGENCY OR THE ABILITY TO HANDLE VARIETY

This is also a topic not usually discussed during reference calls but one that I find to be critical for leadership roles: *How would you rate this person's overall sense of urgency? Please share any specifics that come to mind.* The last thing any one of us wants is to hire someone who needs consistent follow-up and encouragement to push themselves.

On a scale of 0 to 10, where would you rank this person's sense of urgency? Again, scaling helps those who struggle to provide specifics.

The ability for a senior manager to take on multiple projects simultaneously is not optional these days. While there is nothing wrong with those who do a couple of tasks and do them perfectly, if you have a fast-paced growing organization, there is a good chance you are going to need someone who wants to take on more projects and in fact someone who cannot wait to complete the projects so they can move on to the next mission. To get to the bottom of this skill, you could ask, *Is this the type of person who likes to take on one or two things at a time or someone who is likely to have their hands on a lot of different projects?*

TECHNICAL SKILLS

Can you share with me how this person is as a CXO? What are some major projects or initiatives that this person was involved with? The question around projects allows you to best understand the magnitude of impact this candidate had in the previous organization using the technical skills you are hiring for. These questions are not in lieu of any extremely technical question you should have already investigated during the follow-up and case interview steps of the funnel but are intended to corroborate your previously gathered insights. That said, if you wish the referee to give you details on deep technical expertise such as the candidate's coding skills, Lean Six Sigma prowess, or selling abilities, then you should absolutely add them to your list of reference questions.

Did this person identify those initiatives or were those identified by you or someone else senior to the candidate? This question speaks to the candidate's ability to innovate versus their need to be led, managed, or told what to do.

In your opinion can this person be a player if needed? How good of a player can they be for this role? The is an important question for growth stage organizations where the manager sometimes might need to be the player. The candidate's ability to roll up their sleeves to do the technical work can be critical to such companies and in motivating their teams. Whether it is a CFO, CTO, or COO, if they cannot do the real work, then not only do they have a limited ability to manage those who do the work for them, but it may also become tricky to bridge inevitable future transitions on their team.

CHANGE MANAGEMENT SKILLS

Effecting change is the leading catalyst for acquiring top talent. Hence, inquiring about a leader's ability to identify and manage change should be on the top of most reference checks. One way of identifying their skills is by learning about the types, number of, and magnitude of change management projects they were either involved with or led. It speaks to their muscle to work through intense amount of change. *What are some of the major change management projects this person led during their time they worked at your company? What are their top two distinctive traits and two weaknesses as a change leader?*

It is important to understand where in the change process the candidate has relevant experience—specifically, if the candidate is a change agent themselves and will come to you with ideas for improvement or will be relying on you or others in your organization to identify change projects. Questions that can help here include: *Were they involved across the entirety of the process from ideation, design, execution, to realization of outcomes, or only specific parts of it? If the latter, then which parts where they most involved with?* Also, this line of questioning can reveal if they are just identifiers of ideas or if they have the muscle and willingness to implement the changes and see them through to the finish line.

Along the same lines, another way of asking the question would be, *This person is going to be coming to a critical role in our organization, which is going through several changes. Can you share examples of this person's ability to not only adapt to change but also help others in the organization through such change?*

LEADERSHIP STYLE

A major element of diligence for all executive and senior managerial roles—learning about their leadership style—must be a key component of your reference calls. The answer to the questions *How is this person as a leader? Is this someone on whom you relied heavily to provide direction or develop the future strategy of the business, or was that done by you or someone else in the organization?* will allow you to evaluate if the candidate has the leadership and strategic skills needed either as part of their immediate role or in the future or if who you are hiring is going to require significant coaching and mentoring to help them get there.

When this person is leading teams, are the team members likely to be told what to do, or will they experience a more autonomous environment where they get to design and build their own processes and then circle back with the candidate? This speaks to the management style of the candidate and specifically if they rely on prescriptive micromanagement to get things done or prefer a more autonomous approach to leading or managing teams. This attribute can also help you understand the cultural fit within your organization.

Being able to manage projects while keeping them on schedule and within budget is a key skill that simply cannot be deeply tested throughout the recruiting process. The reference call is a great opportunity to learn more regarding this experience. Asking, *Is this person someone who delivers projects or initiatives on time and under budget?* can be very helpful in calibrating their budget management skills.

Many CEOs share that they have leaders (including C-level folks) who come to them with ideas but no facts or plans to back them up. While there should definitely be a place for free flow of ideation, it is unhelpful if that is the only thing you are likely to get from the person you are about to hire. Asking the referee, *For new ideas or opportunities, what type of content or presentation should I expect to see?* can reveal the candidate's ability on presenting operationally viable ideas in their new role. Although the case interview explores the strategy and planning components of the person's skill set, it is no substitute for real-life experience the reference has already had with the candidate.

Building on the last question, you could ask, *Should I expect to receive a detailed business plan, or a work plan, or will I likely see a high-level set of ideas and some basic facts to support it?* This question is critical, specifically for C-level candidates but also for most roles with project management responsibilities. While you will have seen some direct evidence of this during the case interviews, it is helpful to ensure that the candidate has this mindset and approach as part of their practice and that it was not something they did just for the sake of the interview process.

PRIORITIZATION

An employee's need to prioritize is key to their success as they grow within the company. And if you are hiring a manager and particularly a senior executive, then you need them to bring those skills to your team on day one. Ask, *How good is this person at prioritizing?* or, less simply, *How did this person approach prioritization across all the initiatives they were responsible for?* While you may have gotten a taste of this trait through the case interview, it is best to confirm this from the referee, who should be able to give you their experience-based data and insights on how the candidate practically applied this skill in the previous roles.

Finally, you can ask, *Did you find yourself or others in the organization constantly helping the candidate with top priorities or is that something they did on their own and you were kept informed on an as-needed basis?* In case the referee cannot speak to specifics around the candidate's prioritization approach or process, the answer to this question will give you similar data and insights as the previous question.

KEY TAKEAWAYS

✓ You have found the winner, but your diligence is not over yet. The offer should be contingent on finding no red flags in the reference calls.

✓ You, as the CEO, or your talent acquisition champion needs to make as many reference calls as possible to learn the most you can about the candidate.

✓ Get a broad range of feedback that should include supervisors and direct reports but also can include peers.

✓ Pick a handful of topics critical to the role, and tailor your questions to the referee and their likely exposure to the candidate's skills.

✓ Learn about (and validate) areas of distinctiveness and areas of real weakness or blind spots for the candidate. This will allow you to implement the right support structures to make the candidate successful in the job and give you the necessary operating leverage.

CHAPTER 16

PROTECT YOUR INVESTMENT

People don't always tell the entire story, and sometimes when you are trying to quickly close the deal or want someone to start right away, it is hard to pause and do more checks. But for me, doing background checks is not just a no-regret move but a key to ensure I am investing in the right person to join my team. I have been saved by this so many times.

—**RENEE RUMP**, CEO of Heads Up Technologies, USA[1]

AS CEOS, OPERATORS, AND INVESTORS, we are all in the risk management business. Whether we are managing risks around our capital, our customers, or our people, most of what we do is try to ensure that we have the capability to predict, navigate, and hopefully minimize or mitigate the risks. In the same spirit, the main purpose of background checks on the offeree is risk management.

Specifically, the goal with a background check is to make sure there are no skeletons in the offeree's closet that affect not only your team and people but also your company. Fortunately, you don't need to do the heavy lifting; plenty of firms do this for a living. You just need to find one (through your network or simply googling one) to get the job done.

This service, however, is not free, so it is best to wait until after the winner has signed the contingent (to the satisfactory completion of reference calls and background checks) offer letter or employment agreement. This part of the process can start at the same time as you launch into the reference calls. However, some companies are a bit conservative and wish to wait till after the reference checks to ensure the references turn out positive.

One thing to keep in mind is that background checks take up to two weeks to complete, so launching this step as early as possible allows for timely completion of the due diligence on the offeree. The process (for those of you who have not used it before) is straightforward:

- Notify the offeree of the contingency of their offer to this (along with the successful completion of reference calls).
- Identify (if you haven't already) the firm you are going to use for the background check, and source all the appropriate forms to be filled out by the offeree.
- Have them fill out the forms and send those to the background search firm.
- Once the report comes back, go through any flags in detail.
- Have a conversation with the offeree if necessary (in case of any bad surprises).

One thing to keep in mind is that even though you are going to use a firm that specializes in background checks, there is no substitute for good old googling. Sometimes there are topics that do not get picked up by the background checks but are often found on Google searches. Take thirty minutes to google your offeree, or have your recruiting partners (if you have one for this project) do the search for you. All you are looking for are any obvious issues with the candidate, to avoid any surprises about their background.

Some people have brought up the notion of browsing a candidate's social media accounts. My suggestion is to get legal counsel to ensure that all diligence is being conducted in alignment with local privacy laws. The one instance where it may make a lot of sense to look at social media for a candidate is if their portfolio of work (such as for digital and social media marketing roles) is on a professional social media account that the candidate has personally shared, used, and permitted as part of their application for the job.

Examples of some common issues that employers have discovered from background checks include:

- Falsification of education

- Misrepresentation of positions or titles in a job

- Lying about timelines on the resume

- Public safety infringements—especially if the job requires the highest levels of health and safety measures to be followed on-site

- Lawsuits in which the candidate is significantly and currently involved in the process, particularly with a competitor or former employer

Any of these issues is a red flag and worthy of further inquiry or a conversation with your offeree. If there are major issues that could affect the business in the short or long run, you are now able to act on the information at hand. That might mean getting clarification, rescinding the offer and moving on to your backup candidate, or even starting the search process again.

KEY TAKEAWAYS

- ✓ Background checks are primarily a risk mitigation opportunity.

- ✓ Outsource it. A formal background check by a professional third party may be expensive, but it is a lot cheaper than hiring the wrong candidate.

- ✓ Don't ignore the data. If you find any red flags, act on them right away.

CHAPTER 17

FORMALIZE EMPLOYMENT

> As the founder and CEO of a high-growth international tech
> company, I hire top talent at speed and across multiple geographies.
> But one thing we never compromise on is making sure every new
> hire has a formal employment contract before they start. It's how we
> ensure clarity on roles and expectations, and it sets the foundation
> for a strong relationship. In fact, it helps us move at a higher pace
> because we avoid downstream iterations and chaos.
>
> **—CAESAR SENGUPTA**, CEO of Arta Finance, Singapore[1]

FORMALIZATION OF EMPLOYMENT IS simply documenting the verbal agreement between the company and the winning candidate or offeree, on the terms and conditions of employment. This may seem trivial, but a common occurrence many investment firms experience during acquisition diligence is the absence of any record of an employee's offer letter. It is an important document because it symbolizes the beginning of a professional relationship between an employer and an employee. Additionally, it is the one document that the two parties can refer to anytime there is a discrepancy or dispute regarding any form of short- or long-term remuneration issues. Just like the job description, having specifics listed in this document or attached along with the document can be incredibly helpful to resolve future potential conflicts between the parties.

In many cases, especially for senior executives or when long-term incentives are involved, companies may choose to use a legal document or contract that has been blessed by lawyers of both parties. Because these documents can be quite complex and require proper legal analysis, I strongly suggest that, whenever you wish to send a legally binding employment contract, you engage an employment attorney to help draft the language, ensure compliance with state and federal laws, and if necessary, guide the process between the two parties. Additionally, in such circumstances, it is always a good idea to recommend to the offeree that they also engage their own attorney to ensure full understanding of the terms prior to signing the docs.

When it comes to formal engagement letters, the following content (which would and should have previously been agreed on verbally) should always be included by the company.

Title

The job title should be in line with the title used for the job posting, unless the negotiations with the candidate have resulted in a tweak to the title. Either way, this is a key component that should be restated in writing.

Reporting Lines

At this point, your management team should have a clear view of who this role reports to, and where relevant, you can also share the key titles or departments that report to this role.

Start Date

This should be a mutually agreed-on date when the offeree will commence work. This date should allow for any notice periods they have to serve with their current employers as well as any vacation they wish to take prior to commencing employment.

The Type of Contract

The conditions of employment and therefore the compensation require a clear identification of whether the employment being offered is full-time or part-time, on certain days or hours per week. Additionally, in some cases, it may also be important to note whether it is a permanent position or an interim role. In the case of the latter, I strongly recommend that the offer letter also note any potential for conversion from interim to full-time and the conditions under which that might happen. If, however, the company is unwilling to commit to or is unsure of those conditions, then acknowledging the potential of such conversion may be sufficient for the purposes of this agreement.

Annual Base Salary

The annual base salary is the most important item an offeree will look at. They expect to see the same numbers you will have discussed with them throughout the process and particularly during the commit step. The reason I bring this up is that I have come across situations where employers have tried to be a bit cheeky with these numbers, which ended up in a bad surprise for the offeree and upended the entire process. Not to mention the loss of the company's credibility with their future employee and perhaps even in the market. I strongly urge you to double- and triple-check your numbers before sending the offer across. Also, this is a great time and place to highlight specific timelines associated with an employee's annual performance reviews in case any future salary changes are pegged to those reviews.

Bonus and Commissions

In the event of a potential for additional incentives such as bonuses or commissions, these should be clearly included in the offer letter. There are four key items that must be identified to avoid assumptions among the parties. First, for the amount or range, you can either state the maximum potential bonus or commission the employee can earn or a range of bonus outcomes for the year. This should tie back to your assessments during the incentive design step of the Plan stage of the Talent Acquisition Funnel and any subsequent edits based on verbal negotiations with the offeree. Second, whatever the number or range, it is critical that the bonus and commission (where relevant) criteria and calculation methods are clearly explained to the candidate in the offer letter. I have used Excel tables to demonstrate practical scenarios and potential payouts to help the candidates get a good sense of what it would take to achieve the target amounts or fall within the range.

Next, the timing or frequency of bonuses and commissions is important. Depending on your company's policies and the role, these can be paid out quarterly or annually. The payment of these two types of distributions don't have to align. For example, it is perfectly okay for commissions tied to sales (or other monthly metrics) to be paid out at a higher frequency than bonuses. What is most important is that you clearly state when each incentive will get distributed.

Finally, clearly lay out whether the bonus is guaranteed or not. Often employees want to know what their maximum annual salary might look like, as they may be comparing the total compensation package with other competitive offers. Therefore, inform the candidate, via the offer letter, of a clear sense of payout probability of the bonus. Using words such as *contingent* or *discretionary* is important to avoid a false sense of guarantee in the event these distributions are entirely variable. Besides performance, if you have other payout criteria for bonuses, then they should be clearly outlined in this document. Some such scenarios include whether the bonus payouts happen only after the annual audit of company financials, or if the employee needs to be employed at the end of the company's fiscal year, or if there is a full forfeiture of accrued bonus should the employee voluntarily leave during the fiscal year. Whatever the "must have" requirements associated with earning the bonus, outline them in the offer.

Long-Term Incentives

You should have had detailed conversations with the offeree about whether they are getting any long-term incentives and, if so, the amount and type of instrument—equity, options, profits interests, or any other type—they will be receiving. For the purposes of the offer letter, clearly state the final agreed-on elements with their respective eligibility criteria and vesting conditions.

Additionally, I have always found it to be extremely helpful to share a calculation table with the offeree that outlines various plausible scenarios under which the long-term incentives could monetize and generate a positive distribution for the recipient. The fact is that unlike the offeree, who is making an outside-in judgment call on the value of the units, the company will know a lot more about the current value of long-term incentives being offered, future projected or desired valuation of the units, and the likely upside for the person receiving it. Therefore, presenting these details in a clear way and walking the offeree through it will help them appreciate the impact these units could have on their cumulative wealth. A simple outline for this part of the offer letter could include at least the following:

- Long-term incentive type
- Strike price or unit price at the date of offer
- Number of units awarded
- Vesting structure (if relevant)—performance, time, and so on
- Vesting schedule (if relevant)—start date and duration of vesting
- Any other contingencies that affect the above variables

Time Off

You should also include the total number of paid days off, sick leave, and any other form of special leave that the company offers or that has been agreed on during negotiations. Referring to the employee handbook (if there is one) is also a good idea.

Special Working Conditions

Depending on your operating principles and requirements of the role, it is very helpful if your current remote working policies are stated in your formal offer to avoid confusion and debate. Additionally, the office location from which your future employee is required to work should also be clearly stated to ensure future compliance, especially if there is any remuneration tied to such working requirements.

Travel Requirements

Jobs that have travel requirements should have structure and expectations clearly noted in the offer letter. Additionally, it is always helpful if you can share (either in the letter or in an addendum) the travel expense policies and procedures with the offeree.

Benefits

Health care and other (retirement, dental, vision, etc.) benefits are incredibly important compensation components for most employees and a source of competitive advantage for your company. Including all the details of each benefit in an offer letter can be impractical, so once again, a reference to the company's employee handbook and benefits policies in the offer letter is sufficient. The offeree will likely want to see the company policies and understand them in detail. Ideally, connect the offeree directly to your CFO or HR team (whichever is relevant for the company) so they can get all their specific questions answered by those who know the most.

If you have investors on your board, then they can also help you formalize these agreements, given their experience and interest in making sure the financial instruments and terms are accurately reflected. As Josh Finifter, Managing Director at Access Holdings, shared:

As investors, we work through countless contracts, but one of the most important are the employment agreements. To me, it's not just a legal formality but sets the foundation of trust. When written with clarity and consistency, it becomes both a reference point for the future and a foundational document that ensures expectations are aligned and prevents surprises for both parties.[2]

EMOTIONAL INTELLIGENCE

You can continue to validate your offeree's emotional intelligence even during final contract negotiations by paying attention to their behavior and attitude. The data points in table 17.1 are found during compensation negotiations. Their behavior at this stage of the negotiations should simply be noted and, unless there is disqualifying action, this data can help you assess how they may approach negotiations when they are on the other side of the table making offers of employment on behalf of the company or even during external negotiations with clients and vendors.

TABLE 17.1. EQ LEVELS DISPLAYED DURING CLOSE STAGE

EQ attribute or trait	Observations and data points on EQ levels
Respect—self and employer	This can be an uncomfortable dialogue, as both parties are trying to serve their own needs. A high-EQ candidate will handle conflict with professionalism, grace, and kindness.
Thoughtfulness	Ability to understand and appreciate various points of view.
Conflict management	A frustrated or angry approach obviously shows lack of emotional intelligence.
Kindness	A logical, rational, firm but kind approach to joint problem-solving.

With all the above content and anything bespoke to the role included in the offer letter, have the offeree sign the letter and send a copy back to you. You should keep a countersigned letter in your records and share a copy with the offeree. Once this final step is done, the acquisition is complete.

Congratulations! You have technically acquired your preferred talent, and now it's time for the talent to show up to work on the agreed start date and start applying their skills, adding leverage, and generating value for the business. Once they start, the real journey begins as it relates to supporting and developing them to be successful at their job and to retain them in the company.

KEY TAKEAWAYS

- ✓ Formalize all negotiations and discussions (in-person, over the phone, text, or email) by codifying them in writing and presenting them to the winning candidate in an offer letter.

- ✓ From the title to the compensation components and benefits package, every single item important to the company and to the offeree should be clearly detailed in the offer.

- ✓ Share a set of long-term incentive calculations for those receiving them. The offeree knows much less than you do, and the more transparent you can make the offer, the higher the likelihood the candidate will understand the benefits and sign on the dotted line.

CHAPTER 18

STAY CONNECTED

CONGRATULATIONS! YOU JUST COMPLETED the grueling process of hiring the best talent you could find and afford. And hopefully they are equally as excited about working with you and at your company.

Now a cautionary tidbit. Over two decades of hiring people, particularly in operating roles, I can count numerous times when I, other CEOs, and hiring managers wrongfully assumed that once the offeree had formally accepted our offer, we could move on, only to later learn of a gross miscalculation. I have found that, sadly, this is a common and global issue, and it is generally due to insufficient, and at times absent, communication.

The following are some common occurrences and mistakes that I and others have experienced or made after offer acceptance.

- The offeree signed the contract, shook hands, expressed their excitement, but did not show up to work.
- The offeree used their offer to go back to their current employer or another party and ask for more compensation and a better title.

- The company had to push out the start date because of internal issues, creating a lot of space between offer acceptance and the start date, during which the offeree changed their mind or "suddenly" found another opportunity.
- Between the time of the offeree accepting the offer and their start date, there was radio silence from the employer, making the offeree nervous enough to go back out in the market to look for backup opportunities.

While this happens more often in the mid to lower levels in an organization, I have seen it play out firsthand many times with C-level executives, GMs, and functional and department heads. Ultimately, people will and should have the decision rights on their professional journey. That said, at this stage of the game, the last thing any one of us wants is the offeree changing their mind, pushing us into a bit of panic as we try to figure out—what now? Whether it is the cost of an interim resource, the cost of restarting the talent acquisition process, the impact on lost value that would have been generated by the offeree, or simply mental fatigue that comes from the talent acquisition process, the impact on you and your business can be significant.

To manage the above risks and increase the chances of positive returns on our investment, there are two simple things you can do to avoid some of the above issues. First, reduce the amount of time between offer acceptance and the start date. The longer the runway, the more opportunity for noise to infiltrate the offeree's world creating potential for confusion and doubt. Second, immediately after the offer has been accepted, start building a connective tissue between the offeree and the company. Stay connected!

In the words of Mark Sinatra, CEO of Aspen HR, USA:

I think it's a missed opportunity when employers don't stay connected with their new employee who is yet to start. In fact, I think it's dangerous to go radio silent, as there's always a chance that the candidate changes their mind after signing the offer letter because they have not heard anything from the company for a couple of weeks. Act like they are already part of the team, and they will start to feel like they are part of the team even before they show up for their first day at work.[1]

Even though they are not officially on your payroll yet, you should start treating them as if they are. Your mind should have moved forward from acquisition to retention. What better way to retain great talent than to show them that you have already started thinking about their journey with the company. Some of the best ways to stay connected are less about the process (email, phone, etc.) and more about the content. Share new developments with the candidate. Particularly if they are a senior executive, let them know any major bits of news such as the following:

- Revenue- or EBITDA-driving events
- M&A activity
- Addition of new customers
- Raising of new capital
- Revised company valuation
- Launch of a new product or service
- Hiring of other team members

Share materials from recent board documents, financials, marketing presentations, and so on. Invite them to company events; this could be team events, customer events, or any community events that the company organizes. You can also start inviting them to social engagements as well, such as lunch meetings, company happy hours, or team outings.

None of the above efforts need to be limited to executive-level candidates. You should use them for people joining your team across all levels in the organization. If you are truly trying to build one singular positive culture, it should not be limited to the privileged few at the top of the food chain. If anything, it should be for the entire company, and the privileged few at the top should lead the way to take care of all the employees of the organization. For me, talent does not have a specific shape, size, color, gender, nationality, tenure, or title. Talent is, simply put, talent.

KEY TAKEAWAYS

- ✓ Set the start date as close as possible to contract signing to minimize the chances of a change of heart or other surprises.

- ✓ Until the candidate shows up to work, don't assume the process is over.

- ✓ Between the completion of the hiring process and the candidate's start date, stay loosely but meaningfully connected with the person.

✓ Even if they have not started yet, treat them like your team member. Invite them to team or client events, and share general business updates.

IT'S ALL ABOUT PEOPLE!

AS I SAID AT THE START, for me, it always has and always will be about our people. They are the most important assets in any organization. Bringing the right people together is the essential first step to create high-performing teams that will deliver on the vision of the company.

By accepting a position, new employees commit to the company's goals at the risk of other opportunities. Then they show up every day, working hard at their jobs with the intention of bringing their A game. I honestly believe that most if not all folks want and try to be the best they can be throughout their day and especially at work. Without them, there is no product, no service, no growth, and no impact. Whether you are a CEO, a founder, or an investor, it is a true privilege to have people work hard in support of your vision and a common goal.

I wrote this book for two reasons. First, I want you and your company to avoid some of the challenges I faced and the mistakes

I made when it came to acquiring talent. Second, I want to share my Talent Acquisition Funnel (TAF) and operating principles (refer to figure I.1) so that you too can consistently acquire talent, with clarity and speed, in alignment with your company's growth strategy. This structured, simple, and field-tested approach will help you accelerate your company's enterprise value.

Each of the four stages of the TAF and their respective steps were designed to help you get clarity across critical elements in acquiring talent. Your readiness in the Plan stage helped you gain clarity on *what* you were solving for as a business, *why* you needed the people you thought you did, and *when* those folks had to be in their positions. This informed the Prepare stage—the timing for the launch of your individual job-level search process and *who* you needed on your team to help you get to the finish line. The Execute stage gave you everything you needed to implement a systematic, consistent, and scalable process to find your top talent. Finally, in the Close stage, you finished strong by confirming and acquiring the most important asset for your business, your people!

Once your new talent is acquired, the next journey begins for both you, as the employer, and the talent, as the new employee. A range of key issues become extremely important after the acquisition.

Retention

Understanding how to measure employee retention, including differentiating between good and bad retention loss and evaluating the annual cost (real and opportunity) of bad retention loss will inform your development of retention strategies. Developing a culture of good retention and holding management accountable for retention losses will allow you to convert retention practices into a competitive advantage, which will have flow-on effects for rapidly scaling your business.

Performance Management

Cultivating high-performing talent to achieve peak performance requires inspirational leadership as well as a structured performance management approach. Taking job (purpose) descriptions and translating them to performance goals, identifying key performance metrics, calibrating with role and project specific timelines, measuring and reporting those metrics to ensure alignment and transparency, and eventually utilizing them to monitor, reward, and coach talent is all part of a strong performance management system and culture within companies.

Professional Development

Utilizing performance goals and gaps to continue investing in the professional development of talent not only is the right thing to do but also can serve as a powerful retention tool. Continuous performance development of top talent leads to a high-performance culture, which, in turn, creates enormous enterprise value for your company.

Coaching and Mentoring

Depending on the values, strategy, and business model, if you choose to actively coach and mentor your people across all levels in the organization, you can create a systematic talent improvement program for your employees. Done in conjunction with performance management and professional development programs, this initiative can yield enormous benefits for your organization and its people!

———

I think it is important to acknowledge the complexity of the topic of human capital. As much as I would love to get into the specifics of each of the above topics, I can't do them justice in this book. While this book focuses on the strategic and tactical aspects of talent acquisition, my hope is that it also provides you with ideas and practices around the bigger topic of *people*. At the end of the day, I strongly believe that as CEOs, operators, and investors, our job is to find and acquire great people, give them the right tools and coaching to become even better, and then simply get out of their way to let them do the job they were hired to do. If we do that, we will succeed in building great companies.

I am genuinely very excited to have been able to share this book with you and trust it will help you find the talent you need to help achieve the vision and goals of your companies and investments. I am also humbled and honored that you read this book. Whether you implement the entire TAF or just select specific modules that suit your company best, I thank you for allowing me and the TAF to be part of your talent acquisition journey. I look forward to hearing about your journeys and ideas as you continue to build your companies and fulfill your goals and aspirations. You can contact me via my website, at www.rohit-bassi.com.

NOTES

CHAPTER 1

1. Amit Shah, interview by the author, March 9, 2024.

2. Vance Chang, interview by the author, August 28, 2025.

CHAPTER 2

1. David Brown, interview by the author, June 25, 2024.

2. Jorge Gross, interview by the author, August 8, 2024.

3. Pam Vona, interview by the author, December 28, 2024.

CHAPTER 3

1. Caesar Sengupta, interview by the author, December 20, 2024.

2. Natasha DesRuisseaux, interview by the author, May 23, 2024.

3. Josh Finifter, discussion with the author, September 16, 2025.

4. Zack Stiefler, discussion with the author, August 15, 2023.

CHAPTER 4

1. Nick Saunders, interview by the author, May 2, 2024.

2. Adam Cooper, interview by the author, December 6, 2024.

CHAPTER 5

1. Mark Sinatra, interview by the author, March 9, 2024.

2. Renee Rump, interview by the author, July 25, 2024.

CHAPTER 6

1. Samantha Foster, interview by the author, June 20, 2024.
2. Zack Stiefler, discussion with the author, August 15, 2023.

CHAPTER 7

1. Ankit Shah, interview by the author, July 13, 2024.
2. Shana Plott, interview by the author, April 25, 2024.

CHAPTER 8

1. Eric Biro, interview by the author, June 27, 2024.

CHAPTER 9

1. Josh Finifter, discussion with the author, September 16, 2025.
2. Pam Vona, interview by the author, December 28, 2024.

CHAPTER 10

1. Israel Niezen, interview by the author, March 7, 2024.
2. Nancy Splaine, interview by the author, July 4, 2024.
3. Ankit Shah, interview by the author, July 13, 2024.

CHAPTER 11

1. Mark Sinatra, interview by the author, March 9, 2024.
2. Nancy Splaine, interview by the author, July 4, 2024.
3. David Brown, interview by the author, June 25, 2024.

CHAPTER 12

1. Karoon Monfared, interview by the author, April 17, 2024.
2. Amit Shah, interview by the author, March 9, 2024.

CHAPTER 13

1. Samantha Foster, interview by the author, June 20, 2024.

CHAPTER 14

1. Adam Cooper, interview by the author, December 6, 2024.

CHAPTER 15

1. Jorge Gross, interview by the author, August 8, 2024.

2. Karoon Monfared, interview by the author, March 9, 2024.

CHAPTER 16

1. Renee Rump, interview by the author, July 25, 2024.

CHAPTER 17

1. Caesar Sengupta, interview by the author, December 20, 2024.

2. Josh Finifter, discussion with the author, September 16, 2025.

CHAPTER 18

1. Mark Sinatra, interview by the author, March 9, 2024.

INDEX

ABOUT THE AUTHOR

A global citizen who has lived in seven countries across both hemispheres, **ROHIT BASSI** has a deep appreciation for cultural diversity and a lifelong passion for people. He believes people are every organization's most powerful asset—and that companies win when they consistently invest in their people systems.

A private equity veteran, an engineer, and a Wharton MBA, Rohit began his career in McKinsey and Company's private equity practice before becoming both an operator and an investor. He has run, scaled, advised, and sold businesses ranging from small enterprises to those with several hundred million dollars in revenue, and with employee head counts in the thousands across local, national, and international markets.

These experiences inspired him to found People Quotient (PQ), a tech-enabled organizational excellence firm, and to host the *People*

Quotient podcast, where global CEOs and investors share how they build companies and scale high-performing teams.

Exclusive Resource for Readers

Scan below to access your free implementation resource:

9 781639 081653